The Best Liberal Quotes Ever

Why the Left Is Right

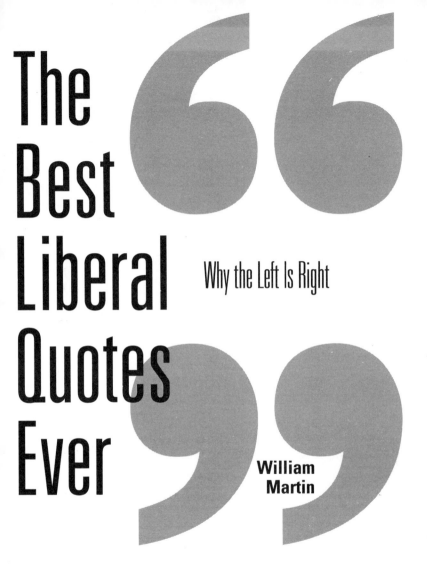

William Martin

SOURCEBOOKS, INC.®
NAPERVILLE, ILLINOIS

Published by Sourcebooks, Inc.
P.O. Box 4410, Naperville, Illinois 60567-4410
(630) 961-3900
FAX: (630) 961-2168
www.sourcebooks.com

Library of Congress Cataloging-in-Publication Data

The best liberal quotes ever : why the left is right / [compiled by]
 William P. Martin.
    p. cm.
 ISBN 1-4022-0309-8 (alk. paper)
 1. Quotations, English. I. Martin, William P.
 PN6081.B45 2004
 081--dc22

                                                      2004012633

               Printed and bound in the United States of America
                    BG 10 9 8 7 6 5 4 3 2 1

These quotations are for my son Matt, my daughter Casey, and my wife Marianne, who mean everything to me.

The book is also dedicated to memory of my parents William and Nancy Martin, who taught me the simple truth that politics should not be about protecting the interests of the rich and powerful, but about helping those who can't help themselves.

TABLE OF CONTENTS

Shocking and Stupid Quotations of the Right

INTRODUCTION

The Best Liberal Quotes Ever: Why the Left is Right is a proud exposition of the wisdom, richness, and diversity of progressive thought. Packed with over 2,000 quotations, it is the most comprehensive collection of liberal quotations ever published. Full of humor, insight, and inspiration, it is a book for open minds and generous hearts. On a variety of fronts, it is also a resource for fighting back—from defending women's basic reproductive rights, to recognizing same-sex marriage, to protecting the environment, to protesting against an unjust war. Featuring a section entitled "Shocking and Stupid Quotations of the Right," *The Best Liberal Quotes Ever* is also a wake-up call about the growing militancy and extremism of the Radical Right.

The Best Liberal Quotes Ever is not a book for racists, misogynists, bigots, chauvinists, gay bashers, warmongers, religious fanatics, gun nuts, fear brokers, anti-abortion extremists, corporate fat cats, or other powerful interests who so fervently identify with the Republican Party. This collection of quotations is for the rest of us.

Who exactly are "the rest of us"? Well, several types of people come to mind—activists, actors, agnostics, aliens, artists, atheists, bohemians, civil libertarians, comedians, contrarians, critics, deists, Democrats, detainees, differently ableds, doubters, environmentalists, evolutionists, existentialists, feminists, free thinkers, gadflies, gays, Greens, gurus, heathens, heretics, hermits, hippies, humanists, idealists, independents, individualists, infidels, intellectuals, lesbians, librarians, liberals, loners, lovers, mavericks, musicians, nonbelievers, nonconformists, outcasts, outsiders, pacifists, pagans, persons of color, philosophers, pluralists, poets, progressives, protesters, radicals, readers, revolutionaries, romantics, saints, secularists, seniors, sinners, skeptics, socialists, teachers, theists, therapists, thinkers, trouble makers, union members, Unitarian-Universalists, utopians, vegetarians, visionaries, volunteers, wanderers, women, and writers.

Selecting the best quotations for this progressive *mélange* was a labor of love guided by the belief that liberalism is more a range of virtues than a formal creed. Quotations were not necessarily selected because a liberal uttered them, but because they exemplified a tendency toward a core virtue such as liberty, equality, or nonviolence. At its best, the spirit of liberalism is the spirit of inclusiveness. We liberals seek truth in a variety of ways and places.

While I bear sole responsibility for this project, I want to thank my friends and colleagues in the Pennsylvania state government for their direct and indirect help. Special thanks to Lance Simmens, Uma Ramaswamy, Glenn Florence, Cindy Presley, Molly Dougherty, Jim Kreider, Paul Hindmarsh, Melia Belonus, Bill Dolbow, Rich Whorl, and Debbie Blackburn. I am particularly grateful to my family—Marianne, Matt, and Casey—for their own liberality and enthusiastic support.

William Martin, Ed.D.
April 2004

The Best
Liberal Quotes
Ever

ACTIVISM

To accomplish great things, we must not only act, but also dream.
—Anatole France

People often say with pride, "I'm not interested in politics." They might as well say, "I'm not interested in my standard of living, my health, my job, my rights, my freedoms, my future, or any future."
—Martha Gellhorn

The hands that help are better far than the lips that pray.
—Robert Ingersoll

Pray for the dead and fight like hell for the living!
—Mother Jones

Stay bored and government becomes more of an instrument of the rich and powerful against the rest of America. Get active with your fellow citizens and you might just see more government of, by, and for the people.
—Ralph Nader

What you don't do can be a destructive force.
—Eleanor Roosevelt

AFRICAN AMERICAN

It comes as a great shock…to discover that the flag to which you
have pledged allegiance…has not pledged allegiance to you. It
comes as a great shock to see Gary Cooper killing off the Indians, and
although you are rooting for Gary Cooper, that the Indians are you.
—James Baldwin

It is ironic that America, with its history of injustice
to the poor, especially the black man and the Indian,
prides itself on being a Christian nation.
—James Cone

I believe that all men, black, brown, and white, are brothers.
—W. E. B. DuBois

I hear that melting-pot stuff a lot, and
all I can say is that we haven't melted.
—Jesse Jackson

The burden of being black is that you
have to be superior just to be equal.
—Jesse Jackson

Black people have always been America's
wilderness in search of a promised land.
—Cornel West

Afrocentricity is simple. If you examine the phenomena
concerning African people, you must give them agency.
If you don't, you're imposing Eurocentrism on them.
—Molefi Assante

AGING

The age of a person doesn't matter. The sweetest
music is played on the oldest violin.
—Jessie Andrews

There is only one solution if old age is not to be an
absurd parody of our former life, and that is to go on
pursuing ends that give our existence a meaning.
—Simone de Beauvoir

When our memories outweigh our dreams, we become old.
—Bill Clinton

A man has made at least a start on discovering the
meaning of human life when he plants shade trees
under which he knows full well he will never sit.
—D. Elton Trueblood

ALIENATION

How does it feel to be on your own, with no direction
home, like a complete unknown, like a rolling stone?
—Bob Dylan

The trouble with me is that I'm an outsider. And
that's a very hard thing to be in American life.
—Jacqueline Kennedy Onassis

Alienation as we find it in modern society is almost total…. Man
has created a world of man-made things as it never existed before.
He has constructed a complicated social machine to administer
the technical machine he built. The more powerful and gigantic
the forces are which he unleashes, the more powerless he
feels himself as a human being. He is owned by his own
creations, and has lost ownership of himself.
—Erich Fromm

Any situation in which some men prevent others from engaging in the process of inquiry is one of violence;...to alienate humans from their own decision making is to change them into objects.
—Paulo Freire

The overall impact of postmodernism is that many other groups now share with black folks a sense of deep alienation, despair, uncertainty, loss of sense of grounding, even if it is not informed by shared circumstance.
—bell hooks

AMERICA

I love America because it is a confused, chaotic mess— and I hope we can keep it this way for at least another thousand years. The permissive society is the free society.
—Edward Abbey

America did not invent human rights. In a very real sense...human rights invented America.
—Jimmy Carter

We hold these Truths to be self-evident, that all Men
are created equal, that they are endowed by their
Creator with certain unalienable Rights, that among
these are Life, Liberty, and the Pursuit of Happiness.
—Declaration of Independence

America was not built by conformists, but by mutineers.
—Jim Hightower

Rank imperialism and warmongering are not American
traditions or values. We do not need to dominate the world.
—Molly Ivins

The white, the Hispanic, the black, the Arab, the Jew, the woman,
the Native American, the small farmer, the businessperson, the
environmentalist, the peace activist, the young, the old, the
lesbian, the gay, and the disabled make up the American quilt.
—Jesse Jackson

I hope ever to see America among the
foremost nations of justice and liberality.
—George Washington

This nation cannot afford to be materially rich and spiritually poor.
—John F. Kennedy

Give me your tired, your poor, your huddled
masses yearning to breathe free.
—Emma Lazarus

America will never be destroyed from the outside. If we falter and
lose our freedoms, it will be because we destroyed ourselves.
—Abraham Lincoln

What the people want is very simple. They want an America as
good as its promise.
—Barbara Jordan

America is great because America is good, and if America
ever ceases to be good, America will cease to be great.
—Alexis de Tocqueville

I look forward to a great future for America—a future in which our
country will match its military strength with our moral restraint, its
wealth with our wisdom, its power with our purpose.
—John F. Kennedy

ANGER

Never forget what a man says to you when he is angry.
—Henry Ward Beecher

In a controversy, the instant we feel anger we have already ceased
striving for the truth, and have begun striving for ourselves.
—Thomas Carlyle

When anger rises, think of the consequences.
—Confucius

When anger spreads through the breast,
guard thy tongue from barking idly.
—Sappho

ANIMAL RIGHTS & VEGETARIANISM

The question is not, "Can they reason?" nor
"Can they talk?" But rather, "Can they suffer?"
—Jeremy Bentham

When nonvegetarians say "human problems come first" I cannot help wondering what exactly it is that they are doing for humans that compels them to continue to support the wasteful, ruthless exploitation of farm animals.
—Peter Singer

True human goodness, in all its purity and freedom, can come to fore only when its recipient has no power. Humanity's true moral test, its fundamental test, consists of its attitude towards those who are at its mercy: animals.
—Milan Kundera

Animals are my friends…and I don't eat my friends.
—George Bernard Shaw

If slaughterhouses had glass walls, everyone would be vegetarian.
—Paul McCartney

The animals of the world exist for their own reasons. They were not made for humans any more than black people were made for whites, or women for men.
—Alice Walker

If children are permitted to be cruel to their pets and other animals, they easily learn to get the same pleasure from the misery of fellow humans. Such tendencies can easily lead to crime.

—Fred A. McGrand

I have from an early age abjured the use of meat, and the time will come when men such as I will look upon the murder of animals as they now look upon the murder of men.

—Leonardo da Vinci

Compassion for animals is intimately connected with goodness of character; and it may be confidently asserted that he who is cruel to animals cannot be a good man.

—Arthur Schopenhauer

ANTI-INTELLECTUALISM

It is ironic that the United States should have been founded by intellectuals, for throughout most of our political history, the intellectual has been for the most part either an outsider, a servant, or a scapegoat.

—Richard Hofstadter

Anti-intellectualism has long been the
anti-Semitism of the businessman.
—Arthur Schlesinger, Jr.

Anti-intellectualism has been a constant thread winding
its way through our political and cultural life, nurtured
by the false notion that democracy means that "my
ignorance is just as good as your knowledge."
—Isaac Asimov

We can no longer tolerate anti-intellectualism. We can no
longer tolerate liberal-bashing and we can no longer
tolerate the politics of the dumb and the mean.
—Janeane Garofalo

American politics are deeply contradictory of course, but anti-
intellectualism…is the common strain. This includes a deep
suspicion of anything that isn't simple, fundamental, traditional,
down-to-earth and "American" in the ideological sense, and can be
exploited easily by demagogues and cynical politicians of the right.
—Edward Said

That which the fascists hate, above all else, is intelligence.
—Miguel de Unamuno

APATHY

The world is a dangerous place to live, not because
of the people who are evil, but because of the
people who don't do anything about it.
—Albert Einstein

The death of democracy is not likely to be an
assassination from ambush. It will be a slow extinction
from apathy, indifference, and undernourishment.
—Robert Maynard Hutchins

If moderation is a fault, then indifference is a crime.
—Jack Kerouac

Apathy can be overcome by enthusiasm, and enthusiasm
can only be aroused by two things: first, an ideal, which
takes the imagination by storm, and second, a definite
intelligible plan for carrying that ideal into practice.
—Arnold J. Toynbee

ATHEISM & AGNOSTICISM

No agnostic ever burned anyone at the stake or
tortured a pagan, a heretic, or an unbeliever.
—Daniel J. Boorstin

I do not consider it an insult, but rather a compliment to be
called an agnostic. I do not pretend to know where many
ignorant men are sure—that is all that agnosticism means.
—Clarence Darrow

It does no injury for my neighbor to say
there are twenty gods or no God.
—Thomas Jefferson

I wanted to become an atheist but I gave it up. They have no
holidays.
—Henny Youngman

The Christian god may exist; so may the gods of Olympus,
or of ancient Egypt, or of Babylon. But no one of these
hypotheses is more probable than any other.
—Bertrand Russell

I have never seen atheism dry the tears of a widowed bride. I have never seen atheism comfort the single mother. I have never seen atheism calm the spirit of a distressed father. And I have never seen atheism offer hope to the hopeless, forgiveness to the sinner, and grace and mercy to all who ask it.
—Logan McAdams

My atheism…is true piety towards the universe and denies only gods fashioned by men in their own image to be servants of their human interests.
—George Santayana

Agnosticism simply means that a man shall not say he knows or believes that for which he has no grounds for professing to believe.
—Thomas Henry Huxley

AUTHORITY

The disappearance of a sense of responsibility is the most far-reaching consequence of submission to authority.
—Stanley Milgram

I believe in a lively disrespect for most forms of authority.
—Rita Mae Brown

If you obey all the rules you will miss the fun.
—Katherine Hepburn

Historically, the most terrible things—war, genocide, and slavery—have resulted not from disobedience, but from obedience.
—Howard Zinn

We believe in the authority of reason and conscience. The ultimate arbiter in religion is not a church, or a document, or an official, but the personal choice and decision of the individual.
—David O. Rankin

BELIEF

I believe in using words, not fists….I believe in my outrage knowing people are living in boxes on the street. I believe in honesty. I believe in a good time. I believe in good food. I believe in sex.
—Susan Sarandon

Do not believe in anything simply because it is found written in
your religious books. Do not believe in anything merely on the
authority of your teachers and elders. Do not believe in traditions
because they have been handed down for many generations. But
after observation and analysis, when you find that anything
agrees with reason and is conducive to the good and benefit
of one and all, then accept it and live up to it.
—Buddha

The price of seeking to force our beliefs on others is
that someday they might force their beliefs on us.
—Mario Cuomo

The trouble is that not enough people have come together with the
firm determination to live the things which they say they believe in.
—Eleanor Roosevelt

What is wanted is not the will to believe, but the
will to find out, which is the exact opposite.
—Bertrand Russell

At the core of all well-founded belief, lies belief that is unfounded.
—Ludwig Wittgenstein

What a person believes is not as
important as how a person believes.
—Timothy Virkkala

Those who can make you believe absurdities
can make you commit atrocities.
—François Voltaire

BIBLE

Make your own bible. Select and collect all the
words and sentences that in all your readings
have been to you like the blast of a trumpet.
—Ralph Waldo Emerson

Beware the man of a single book.
—Bertrand Russell

While reading the Ten Commandments is great, living
them is even better—particularly the biblical
admonition about tending to the least among us.
—Arianna Huffington

The Bible is literature, not dogma.
—George Santayana

The Bible among other books is as a diamond among precious stones.
—John Stoughton

There are more scriptural reasons to oppose
homophobia than to oppose homosexuality.
—John B. Cobb

BIGOTRY & PREJUDICE

Prejudice is a raft onto which the shipwrecked
mind clambers and paddles to safety.
—Ben Hecht

Prejudices are what fools use for reason.
—François Voltaire

The mind of a bigot is like the pupil of an eye. The
more light you shine on it, the more it will contract.
—Oliver Wendell Homes

You can safely assume that you've created God in your own image
when it turns out that God hates all the same people you do.

—Anne Lamott

It is never too late to give up your prejudices.

—Henry David Thoreau

I believe in an America where religious intolerance will
someday end…where every man has the same right
to attend or not attend the church of his choice.

—John F. Kennedy

BOOKS

When I get a little money I buy books;
and if any is left I buy food and clothes.

—Erasmus

Read, every day, something no one else is reading.
Think, every day, something no one else is thinking….
It is bad for the mind to be always part of unanimity.

—Christopher Morley

I think we ought to read only the kind
of books that wound and stab us.
—Franz Kafka

All books are either dreams or swords.
—Amy Lowell

The lover of books is a miner, searching for gold all his life long.
—Katherine Peterson

I believe I belong to the last literary generation, the last
generation, that is, for whom books are a religion.
—Erica Jong

A classic is something that everybody wants
to have read and nobody wants to read.
—Mark Twain

BUSH, GEORGE W.

Bush wasn't elected, he was selected? Selected by five
judges up in Washington who voted along party lines.
—Alec Baldwin

I think it is nothing short of unbelievable that the governor of a major state [George W. Bush] running for president thought it was acceptable to mock a woman he decided to put to death.

—Gary Bauer

George W. Bush is a liar. He has lied large and small. He has lied directly and by omission. He has misstated facts, knowingly or not. He has misled. He has broken promises, been unfaithful to political vows. Through his campaign for the presidency and his first years in the White House, he has mugged the truth not merely in honest error, but deliberately, consistently, and repeatedly to advance his career and his agenda.

—David Corn

The evidence is overwhelming that George W. Bush and Richard B. Cheney have engaged in deceit and deception over going to war in Iraq. This is an impeachable offense.

—John Dean

Bush's lies now fill volumes. He lied us into two hideously unfair tax cuts; he lied us into an unnecessary war with disastrous consequences; he lied us into the Patriot Act, eviscerating our freedoms.

—Molly Ivins

I'm absolutely delighted that Senator Kerry has emerged as the front runner, because a war hero who wants to use military force only as the last resort stacks up very well against a warmonger who has not experienced war personally.
—George Soros

The things that President Bush can't find: the White House leak, weapons of mass destruction in Iraq, Saddam Hussein, Osama bin Laden, a link between Saddam Hussein and Osama bin Laden, the guy who sent the anthrax through the mail, and his own butt with two hands and a flashlight.
—Tina Fey

He's probably the least qualified person ever to be nominated by a major party…. What's his accomplishment? That he's no longer an obnoxious drunk?
—Ron Reagan, Jr.

I could never be the president. Think about it. I've abused cocaine, I've been arrested, I'm not a very smart guy. It's a big joke to think people would want someone like me…just because my dad was president.
—Charlie Sheen

George W. Bush was so indifferent to the world that in the years before he became president he made only two overseas trips, both for business, neither for curiosity. No wonder he wants to break the missile treaty, alienate NATO, ignore global warming, and reinstall Russia and China as enemies—those foreign countries scarcely exist in his imagination. Why go to Australia when you have the Outback Steakhouse right here at home?

—Roger Ebert

I reject George Bush's radical new vision…that turns its back on the very alliances we helped create and the very principles that have made our nation a model to the world for over two centuries.

—John Kerry

The majority of Americans—the ones who never elected you—are not fooled by your weapons of mass distraction.

—Michael Moore

As an actor, I know in my mind, watching him [Bush], what a low-quality mind he has. Because I've been doing this since I was five years old, I know when a person is saying words that aren't their own—and it's apparent as it could possibly be to me that he's a mouthpiece, and not even a good mouthpiece.

—Edward Norton

Here's a guy who was born on third base and thinks he hit a triple.
—Ann Richards

George W. Bush is an odd combination of ridiculous
and dangerous. He's sort of an evil idiot savant.
—Thom Rutledge

It's time to impeach the president and get a
man in there to get us out of this mess.
—Bruce Springsteen

George W. Bush promised us a foreign policy with humility.
Instead, he has brought us humiliation in the eyes of the world.
—Al Gore

CENSORSHIP

Books won't stay banned. They won't burn. Ideas won't go to jail. In
the long run of history, the censor and the inquisitor have always lost.
—A. Whitney Griswold

You can cage the singer but not the song.
—Harry Belafonte

The freedom to read is essential to our democracy. It is continuously under attack. Private groups and public authorities in various parts of the country are working to remove books from sale, to censor textbooks, to label "controversial" books, to distribute lists of "objectionable" books or authors, and to purge libraries.

—American Library Association and Association of American Publishers

You don't have to burn books to destroy a culture.
Just get people to stop reading them.

—Ray Bradbury

Wherever they burn books they will also, in the end, burn people.

—Ralph Waldo Emerson

Freedom of the press is guaranteed only to those who own one.

—A. J. Liebling

One of the curious things about censorship is
that no one seems to want it for himself.

—Edgar Dale

CERTAINTY

Madness is the result not of uncertainty but certainty.
—Friedrich Nietzsche

Tolerance grows only when faith loses
certainty; certainty is murderous.
—Will Durant

The quest for certainty blocks the search for meaning. Uncertainty
is the very condition to impel man to unfold his powers.
—Erich Fromm

Maturity is the capacity to endure uncertainty.
—John Huston Finley

Doubt is not a pleasant mental state, but certainty is a ridiculous one.
—François Voltaire

If a man will begin with certainties, he shall end in doubts; but if
he will be content to begin with doubts, he shall end in certainties.
—Francis Bacon

CHANGE

The main dangers in this life are the people
who want to change everything or nothing.
—Nancy Astor

If there is no transformation inside of us, all the structural
change in the world will have no impact on our institutions.
—Peter Block

There is nothing more difficult to take in hand or
more perilous to conduct…than to take the lead
in the introduction of a new order of things.
—Niccolo Machiavelli

A capacity to change is indispensable. Equally indispensable
is the capacity to hold fast to that which is good.
—John Foster Dulles

Everyone thinks of changing the world, but
no one thinks of changing himself.
—Leo Tolstoy

We must become the change we wish to see in the world.
—Mahatma Gandhi

We must always change, renew, rejuvenate
ourselves; otherwise, we harden.
—Johann von Goethe

When you blame others you give up your power to change.
—Douglas Noel Adams

A revolution is coming—a revolution which will be peaceful
if we are wise enough; compassionate if we care enough;
successful if we are fortunate enough—but a revolution
is coming whether we will it or not. We can affect its
character; we cannot alter its inevitability.
—Robert F. Kennedy

Things do not change, we change.
—Henry David Thoreau

CHARACTER

The greatest of all faults is to be conscious of none.
—Thomas Carlyle

The great hope of society is individual character.
—William Ellery Channing

It is not the brains that matter most, but that which guides them—
the character, the heart, generous qualities, progressive ideas.
—Fyodor Dostoevsky

We do not need to proselytize either by our speech
or by our writing. We can only do so really with our
lives. Let our lives be open books for all to study.
—Mahatma Gandhi

Every man has three characters: that which he shows,
that which he has, and that which he thinks he has.
—Alphonse Karr

Character, not circumstances, makes the man.
—Booker T. Washington

A man never discloses his own character
so clearly as when he describes another's.
—Jean Paul Richter

Be more concerned with your character than your reputation,
because your character is what you really are, while your
reputation is merely what others think you are.
—John Wooden

CHILDREN

The most insidious influence on the young is not violence,
drugs, tobacco, drink, or sexual perversion, but our pursuit
of the trivial and our tolerance of the third rate.
—Eric Anderson

Don't worry that children never listen to you;
worry that they are always watching you.
—Robert Fulghum

There is no such thing as other people's children.
—Hillary Rodham Clinton

The question is not whether we can afford to invest
in every child; it is whether we can afford not to.
—Marian Wright Edelman

Your children are not your children.... For their souls
dwell in the house of tomorrow, which you
cannot visit, not even in your dreams.
—Kahlil Gibran

There is no trust more sacred than the one the world holds with
children. There is no duty more important than ensuring that their
rights are respected, that their welfare is protected, that their lives
are free from fear and want and that they grow up in peace.
—Kofi Annan

It's easier to build strong children than to repair broken men.
—Frederick Douglas

CHURCH-STATE SEPARATION

The United States is not a Christian nation any more
than it is a Jewish or a Mohammedan nation.
—John Adams

I'm completely in favor of the separation of church and state. My idea is that these two institutions screw us up enough on their own, so both of them together is certain death.
—George Carlin

I pledge allegiance to my flag and to the republic for which it stands, one nation, indivisible, with liberty and justice for all.
—Original Pledge of Allegiance

The word "God" does not appear in the Constitution, a document that erects if not quite a wall, at least a fence between church and state.
—Arthur Schlesinger, Jr.

The United States of America should have a foundation free from the influence of clergy.
—George Washington

The United States is not a Christian nation. It is a great nation with Christians, among others, in it. But our greatness is based on the fact that there is no official religion.
—Lowell Weicker

CIVIL LIBERTIES

Liberty is always unfinished business.
—American Civil Liberties Union

He that would make his own liberty secure, must guard
even his enemy from opposition; for if he violates his duty,
he establishes a precedent that will reach to himself.
—Thomas Paine

If the fires of freedom and civil liberties burn low in
other lands they must be made brighter in our own.
—Franklin D. Roosevelt

If America has a civic religion, the First
Amendment is its central article of faith.
—Henry Louis Gates, Jr.

In times of emergency, the first thing to
take a whipping is our civil rights.
—Bruce Springsteen

CIVIL RIGHTS

I am—Somebody. I may be poor, but I am—Somebody!
I may be on welfare, but I am—Somebody! I may be
uneducated, but I am—Somebody! I must be, I'm God's
child. I must be respected and protected. I am black and
I am beautiful! I am—Somebody! Soul Power!
—Jesse Jackson

Nonviolence is a powerful and just weapon…which
cuts without wounding and ennobles the man who
wields it. It is a sword that heals.
—Martin Luther King, Jr.

I have a dream that my four little children will one day live
in a nation where they will not be judged by the color of
their skin, but by the content of their character.
—Martin Luther King, Jr.

There are no "white" or "colored" signs on
the foxholes or graveyards of battle.
—John F. Kennedy

I'm the world's original gradualist. I just
think ninety-odd years is gradual enough.
—Thurgood Marshall

All I was doing was trying to get home from work.
—Rosa Parks

CLASS

The class which has the power to rob upon a large scale has also
the power to control the government and legalize their robbery.
—Eugene V. Debs

The American people have this to learn: that where justice
is denied, where poverty is enforced, where ignorance
prevails, and where any one class is made to feel that
society is an organized conspiracy to oppress, rob, and
degrade them, neither person nor property is safe.
—Frederick Douglass

Class interests are best served when masked as national interests.
—Unknown

The distinctions separating the social classes
are false; in the last analysis they rest on force.
—Albert Einstein

History is the long and tragic story of the fact that privileged
groups seldom give up their privileges voluntarily.
—Martin Luther King, Jr.

The history of all hitherto existing society
is the history of class struggles.
—Karl Marx

COMPASSION

How far you go in life depends on you being tender with the
young, compassionate with the aged, sympathetic with the
striving, and tolerant of the weak and the strong. Because
someday in life you will have been all of these.
—George Washington Carver

Compassion is the chief law of human existence.
—Fyodor Dostoevsky

Before you speak, ask yourself if what you are going to say
is true, is kind, is necessary, is helpful. If the answer is no,
maybe what you are about to say should be left unsaid.
—Bernard Meltzer

It's compassion that makes gods of us.
—Dorothy Gilman

Great opportunities to help others seldom come,
but small ones surround us every day.
—Sally Koch

CONFORMITY

Few, if any, survive their teens. Most surrender to the
vague but murderous pressure of adult conformity.
—Maya Angelou

The reward for conformity is everyone likes you but yourself.
—Rita Mae Brown

Born originals, how comes it to pass that we die copies?
—Edward Young

There are two kinds of men who never amount to much: those who cannot do what they are told, and those who can do nothing else.
—Cyrus Curtis

Every society honors its live conformists
and its dead troublemakers.
—Mignon McLaughlin

May God prevent us from becoming "right-thinking men"—that is to say, men who agree perfectly with their own police.
—Thomas Merton

We are so placid that the smallest tremor of objection
to anything at all is taken as a full-scale revolution.
—Cynthia Ozick

A man must consider what a rich realm he
abdicates when he becomes a conformist.
—Publilius Syrus

Whenever you find yourself on the side of the
majority, it is time to pause and reflect.
—Mark Twain

There are some things in every environment to which no honest man should ever adjust himself.
—Robert Maynard Hutchins

CONSCIENCE

Never do anything against conscience even if the state demands it.
—Albert Einstein

In matters of conscience, the law of majority has no place.
—Mahatma Gandhi

I cannot and will not cut my conscience to fit this year's fashions.
—Lillian Hellman

Conscience is God's presence in man.
—Emanuel Swedenborg

Cowardice asks the question, "Is it safe?" Expediency asks the question, "Is it politic?" Vanity asks the question, "Is it popular?" But conscience asks the question, "Is it right?"
—Martin Luther King, Jr.

If we are to survive, we must have ideas, vision, and courage.
These things are rarely produced by committees. Everything that
matters in our intellectual and moral life begins with an individual
confronting his own mind and conscience in a room by himself.

—Arthur Schlesinger, Jr.

CONSERVATIVES

A conservative young man has wound up his life before it was
unreeled. We expect old men to be conservative, but when a
nation's young men are so, its funeral bell is already rung.

—Henry Ward Beecher

The modern conservative is engaged in one of man's oldest
exercises in moral philosophy; that is, the search for a
superior moral justification for selfishness.

—John Kenneth Galbraith

The conundrum of modern political conservatism is that its
superstitious worship of market forces brings about the disruption
of the very families and communities that it claims to revere.

—Gary Hart

Liberals inhabit a world painted a thousand shades of gray. Conservatives live in a black and white world.
—David Morris

The more men have to lose, the less willing are they to venture.
—Thomas Paine

Conservatives walk backward, pretending it is the future.
—George Seldes

Loyalty to petrified opinions never yet broke a chain or freed a human soul in this world—and never will.
—Mark Twain

A conservative is a man who believes that nothing should be done for the first time.
—Alfred E. Wiggam

All conservatives are such from personal defects. They have been effeminated by position or nature, born halt and blind, through luxury of their parents, and can only, like invalids, act on the defensive.
—Ralph Waldo Emerson

CORPORATE POWER

I see in the near future a crisis approaching that unnerves me and causes me to tremble for the safety of my country…corporations have been enthroned and an era of corruption in high places will follow.
—Abraham Lincoln

The most effective way to restrict democracy is to transfer decision-making from the public arena to unaccountable institutions: kings and princes, priestly castes, military juntas, party dictatorships, or modern corporations.
—Noam Chomsky

CORPORATION, n: An ingenious device for obtaining individual profit without individual responsibility.
—Ambrose Bierce

The term "free market" is really a euphemism. What the far right actually means by this term is "lawless market." In a lawless market, entrepreneurs can get away with privatizing the benefits of the market (profits), while socializing its costs (like pollution).
—Steve Kangas

I hope that we shall crush in its birth the aristocracy of our monied corporations which dare already to challenge our government to a trial of strength, and bid defiance to the laws of our country.
—Thomas Jefferson

Behind the ostensible government sits enthroned an invisible government owing no allegiance and acknowledging no responsibility to the people. To destroy this invisible government, to befoul the unholy alliance between corrupt business and corrupt politics is the first task of the statesmanship of the day.
—Theodore Roosevelt

The corporations don't have to lobby the government anymore. They are the government.
—Jim Hightower

Talk of democracy has little content when big business rules the life of the country through its control of the means of production, exchange, the press and other means of publicity, propaganda, and communication.
—John Dewey

COURAGE

The ultimate measure of a man is not where he stands in moments of comfort and convenience, but where he stands at times of challenge and controversy.
—Martin Luther King, Jr.

Courage is a special kind of knowledge. It's knowing how to fear what you ought to fear and how not to fear what you ought not fear.
—David Ben-Gurion

Few are willing to brave the disapproval of their fellows, the censure of their colleagues, the wrath of their society. Moral courage is a rarer commodity than bravery in battle or great intelligence.
—Robert F. Kennedy

Life shrinks or expands in proportion to one's courage.
—Anaïs Nin

A ship in harbour is safe, but that is not what ships are built for.
—John A. Shedd

Courage is the greatest of all the virtues. Because if you haven't courage, you may not have an opportunity to use any of the others.
—Samuel Johnson

All serious daring starts from within.
—Eudora Welty

It takes courage to believe, and it takes courage not to, and who is to say which is the deeper and more truthful?
—Herbert Weisinger

It is curious; curious that physical courage should be so common in the world, and moral courage so rare.
—Mark Twain

I swore never to be silent whenever and wherever human beings endure suffering and humiliation. We must always take sides. Neutrality helps the oppressor, never the victim. Silence encourages the tormentor, never the tormented.
—Elie Wiesel

CRIME

The degree of civilization in a society can
be judged by entering its prisons.
—Fyodor Dostoevsky

The law does not content itself with classifying
and punishing crime. It invents crime.
—Norman Douglas

Crime is naught but misdirected energy.
—Emma Goldman

Perhaps I am too cynical, but I believe there is a separate class
of people in this country called Too Rich to Go to Prison.
—Molly Ivins

Every time you stop a school, you will have to build a jail.
What you gain at one end you lose at the other. It's like
feeding a dog on his own tail. It won't fatten the dog.
—Mark Twain

We make our own criminals, and their crimes are congruent with the national culture we all share.
—Margaret Mead

Crime is a logical extension of the sort of behavior that is often considered perfectly respectable in legitimate business.
—Robert Rice

We have a criminal jury system which is superior to any in the world; and its efficiency is only marred by the difficulty of finding twelve men every day who don't know anything and can't read.
—Mark Twain

Great is the mischief of legal crime.
—Ralph Waldo Emerson

CULTURE

No culture can live, if it attempts to be exclusive.
—Mahatma Gandhi

To appreciate the noble is a gain which can never be torn from us.
—Johann von Goethe

That is true culture which helps us to work
for the social betterment of all.
—Henry Ward Beecher

We are in the process of creating what deserves to be called the
idiot culture.... For the first time, the weird and the stupid and the
coarse are becoming our cultural norm, even our cultural ideal.
—Carl Bernstein

The true civilization is where every man gives to
every other every right that he claims for himself.
—Robert Ingersoll

There is no hierarchy of values by which one culture has the
right to insist on its own values and deny those of another.
—Margaret Mead

DEATH PENALTY

Until the infallibility of human judgment shall have been proved to
me, I shall persist in demanding the abolition of the death penalty,
—Marquis de Lafayette

If we are not our brother's keeper, let us
at least not be his executioner.
—Marlon Brando

A system that will take life must first give justice.
—John J. Curtin, Jr.

The death penalty is reserved for people who do
not have enough money to defend themselves.
—Paul Simon

DEMOCRACY

We cannot use a double standard for measuring our own
and other people's policies. Our demands for democratic
practices in other lands will be no more effective than
the guarantees of those practiced in our own country.
—Hubert H. Humphrey

We can have a democratic society or we can
have the concentration of great wealth in the
hands of the few. We cannot have both.
—Louis Brandeis

Democracy is created by making an aggressive, determined,
and long-term effort at eradicating the real axis of evil:
poverty, homelessness, no health care.
—Tony Kushner

You measure democracy by the freedom it gives its dissidents,
not the freedom it gives its assimilated conformists.
—Abbie Hoffman

An article of the democratic faith is that
greatness lies in each person.
—Bill Bradley

Democracy belongs to those who exercise it.
—Bill Moyers

Democracy is a process by which the people are
free to choose the man who will get the blame.
—Laurence J. Peter

The punishment which the wise suffer who refuse to take part in
the government, is to live under the government of worse men.
—Plato

A free society is one where it is safe to be unpopular.
—Adlai Stevenson

Every kind of peaceful cooperation among men is primarily
based on mutual trust and only secondarily on institutions
such as courts of justice and police.
—Albert Einstein

DEMOCRATS

The Democrats seem to be basically nicer people, but
they have demonstrated time and again that they
have the management skills of celery.
—Dave Barry

I want to make one thing clear: I'm pro-choice, I'm pro-affirmative
action, I'm pro-environment, pro-health care, and pro-labor. And if
that ain't a Democrat, then I must be at the wrong meeting.
—Wesley Clark

America does not need two Republican parties.
—John Kerry

Democrats don't need to add the word compassionate to further
define what they are: the notion is already built in to the philosophy.
—Alan Colmes

I'm here to represent the Democratic wing of the Democratic Party.
—Howard Dean

The greatest leaders in fighting for an integrated America in the
twentieth century were in the Democratic Party. The fact is, it was
the liberal wing of the Democratic Party that ended segregation.
—Newt Gingrich

Some people say we need a third party. I wish we had a second one.
—Jim Hightower

I belong to no organized political party: I am a Democrat.
—Will Rogers

Democrats are children of the Enlightenment. They
believe in the perfectibility of humanity. They
revere systems even more than they do results.
—Paul Begala

DISABILITIES

The good we secure for ourselves is precarious and uncertain—until it is secured for all of us and incorporated into our common life.
—Jane Addams

Every student can learn, just not on the same day, or the same way.
—George Evans

Rebellion against your handicaps gets you nowhere. Self-pity gets you nowhere. One must have the adventurous daring to accept oneself as a bundle of possibilities and undertake the most interesting game in the world—making the most of one's best.
—Harry Emerson Fosdick

I thank God for my handicaps, for through them, I have found myself, my work, and my God.
—Helen Keller

All of us do not have equal talent, but all of us should have an equal opportunity to develop our talents.
—John F. Kennedy

None can be called deformed but the unkind.
—William Shakespeare

DISSENT

Dissent is the highest form of patriotism.
—Thomas Jefferson

One has a moral responsibility to disobey unjust laws.
—Martin Luther King, Jr.

The dissenter is every human being at those moments of his life
when he resigns momentarily from the herd and thinks for himself.
—Archibald MacLeish

We must not confuse dissent with disloyalty. When the loyal
opposition dies, I think the soul of America dies with it.
—Edward R. Murrow

I have spent many years of my life in
opposition, and I rather like the role.
—Eleanor Roosevelt

Intellect does not attain its full force unless it attacks power.
—Madame de Stael

DIVERSITY & PLURALISM

Diversity…is not polite accommodation. Instead, diversity is, in action, the sometimes painful awareness that other people, other races, other voices, other habits of mind, have as much integrity of being, as much claim on the world as you do.
—William Chase

Ultimately, America's answer to the intolerant man is diversity, the very diversity which our heritage of religious freedom has inspired.
—Robert F. Kennedy

Stupidity is an attempt to iron out all differences, and not to use or value them creatively.
—Bill Mollison

When we lose the right to be different, we lose the privilege to be free.
—Charles Evans Hughes

The plague of mankind is the fear and rejection of diversity:
monotheism, monarchy, monogamy, and, in our age,
monomedicine. The belief that there is only one right way to live,
only one right way to regulate religious, political, sexual,
medical affairs is the root cause of the greatest threat to man.
—Thomas Szasz

Our nation is a rainbow—red, yellow, brown, black,
and white—and we're all precious in God's sight.
—Jesse Jackson

Cultural pluralism: it's the air we breathe; it's the ground we stand on.
—Ralph Ellison

DOUBT

There are two ways to slide easily through life; to believe
everything or doubt everything. Both ways save us from thinking.
—Alfred Korzybski

If you would be a real seeker after truth, it is necessary that at
least once in your life you doubt, as far as possible, all things.
—Rene Descartes

Believe nothing, no matter where you read it, or who said it, no matter if I have said it, unless it agrees with your own reason and your own common sense.
—Buddha

Freedom of speech and freedom of action are meaningless without freedom to think. And there is no freedom of thought without doubt.
—Bergen Evans

Humanity's first sin was faith; the first virtue was doubt.
—Mike Huben

I respect faith, but doubt is what gets you an education.
—Wilson Mizner

I am an agnostic pagan. I doubt the existence of many gods.
—Unknown

I think we ought always to entertain our opinions with some measure of doubt. I shouldn't wish people dogmatically to believe any philosophy, not even mine.
—Bertrand Russell

ECONOMIC JUSTICE

The "trickle-down" theory: the principle that the poor,
who must subsist on table scraps dropped by the rich,
can best be served by giving the rich bigger meals.
—William Blum

We do not have a money problem in America.
We have a values and priorities problem.
—Marian Wright Edelman

One function of the income gap is that the people at the top of
the heap have a hard time even seeing those at the bottom.
They practically need a telescope. The pharaohs of ancient
Egypt probably didn't waste a lot of time thinking about
the people who built their pyramids, either.
—Molly Ivins

Liberals are not unconcerned with economic liberty, but they have
come to believe that the common good requires that social justice
be given a higher priority than absolute economic freedom.
—Robert S. McElvaine

If we're going to end welfare, the rich should be the first to lose it.
—Mac Morgan

Of course I believe in free enterprise, but in my system of free enterprise, the democratic principle is that there never was, never has been, never will be, room for the ruthless exploitation of the many for the benefit of the few.
—Harry S. Truman

EDUCATION

Only the educated are free.
—Epictetus

Enlighten the people generally, and tyranny and oppression of the body and mind will vanish like evil spirits at the dawn of day.
—Thomas Jefferson

Strong schools are as important to our future as a strong defense.
—Edward M. Kennedy

Intelligence plus character, that is the goal of true education.
—Martin Luther King, Jr.

More money is put into prisons than into schools. That, in itself, is the description of a nation bent on suicide.

—Jonathan Kozol

I wonder how many Einsteins have been permanently discouraged through competitive examinations and the forced feeding of curricula.

—Carl Sagan

Education: the path from cocky ignorance to miserable uncertainty.

—Mark Twain

ENVIRONMENT

What's the use of a house if you haven't got a tolerable planet to put it on?

—Henry David Thoreau

Anything else you're interested in is not going to happen if you can't breathe the air and drink the water. Don't sit this one out. Do something. You are, by accident of fate, alive at an absolutely critical moment in the history of our planet.

—Carl Sagan

Unless we find a way to dramatically change our civilization and our way of thinking about the relationship between humankind and the earth, our children will inherit a wasteland.
—Al Gore

Feelings that morality has nothing to do with the way you use the resources of the world is an idea that can't persist much longer. If it does, then we won't.
—Barbara Kingsolver

There are no passengers on spaceship earth. We are all crew.
—Marshall McLuhan

I really wonder what gives us the right to wreck this poor planet of ours.
—Kurt Vonnegut

I see the day in our own lifetime that reverence for the natural systems, the oceans, the rainforests, the soil, the grasslands, and all other living things—will be so strong that no narrow ideology based upon politics or economics will overcome it.
—Jerry Brown

EQUALITY

Equality of rights under the law shall not be denied or abridged by
the United States or by any state on account of sex.
—Defeated constitutional amendment

I believe in Liberty for all men: the space to stretch their arms
and their souls; the right to breathe and the right to vote, the
freedom to choose their friends, enjoy the sunshine, and ride
on the railroads, uncursed by color; thinking, dreaming,
working, as they will in a kingdom of God and love.
—W. E. B. DuBois

From the equality of rights springs identity of our highest
interests; you cannot subvert your neighbor's rights
without striking a dangerous blow at your own.
—Carl Schurz

One of the things about equality is not just that you
be treated equally to a man, but that you treat
yourself equally to the way you treat a man.
—Marlo Thomas

Just think—guns have a constitutional amendment
protecting them and women don't.
—Eleanor Smeal

When we talk about equal pay for equal work, women in the
workplace are beginning to catch up. If we keep going at this
current rate, we will achieve full equality in about 475 years.
—Lya Sorano

ETHICS

Here's my Golden Rule for a tarnished age: Be fair with
others but then keep after them until they're fair with you.
—Alan Alda

Ethics should precede economics.... We know this because
we've seen the results of capitalism without conscience: the
pollution of the air we breathe, the water we drink, and the
food we eat; the endangerment of workers; and the sale of
dangerous products—from cars to toys to drugs. All in
pursuit of greater and greater profits.
—Arianna Huffington

The first step in the evolution of ethics is a
sense of solidarity with other human beings.
—Albert Schweitzer

Do all the good you can, by all the means you can, in all
the ways you can, in all the places you can, at all the times
you can, to all the people you can, as long as ever you can.
—John Wesley

Man would indeed be in a poor way if he had to be restrained
by fear of punishment and hope of reward after death.
—Albert Einstein

FAITH

It is true, that a little philosophy inclineth man's mind to atheism,
but depth in philosophy bringeth men's minds about to religion.
—Francis Bacon

Do not seek to follow in the footsteps of
the men of old; seek what they sought.
—Basho

Faith, it seems to me, is not the holding of certain
dogmas; it is simply openness and readiness of the
heart to believe any truth which God may show.
—Margaret Deland

As a Christian, there is no other part of the New Right ideology that
concerns me more than its self-serving misuse of religious faith.
—Mark O. Hatfield

The creed whose legitimacy is most easily challenged is likely to
develop the strongest proselytizing impulse.
—Eric Hoffer

The notion that faith in Christ is to be rewarded by an eternity
of bliss, while a dependence upon reason, observation, and
experience merits everlasting pain, is too absurd for refutation.
—Robert Ingersoll

The invisible and the nonexistent look very much alike.
—Delos McKown

Say what you will about the sweet miracle of unquestioning
faith. I consider the capacity for it terrifying.
—Kurt Vonnegut

FAMILIES

I talk and talk and talk, and I haven't taught people in fifty
years what my father taught by example in one week.
—Mario Cuomo

Unless we work to strengthen the family, to create
conditions under which most parents will stay together,
all the rest, schools, playgrounds, and public assistance,
and private concern, will never be enough.
—Lyndon B. Johnson

Patriarchy's chief institution is the family. It is both a
mirror of and a connection with the larger society; a
patriarchal unit within a patriarchal whole.
—Kate Millett

Right now everyone in the world seems to think that they are
codependent and that they come from dysfunctional families…
I call it the human condition.
—Cynthia Heimel

There's no such thing as fun for the whole family.
—Jerry Seinfeld

FASCISM

What distinguishes the New Right from other American
reactionary movements, and what it shares with the early
phase of German fascism, is its incorporation of conservative
impulses into a system of representation consisting
largely of media techniques and media images.
—Philip Bishop

I am worried that we are going through a kind of antiliberal revolt,
belief in a very strong state, a contempt for pluralism, for a "soft"
welfare state, and a sense that we cannot afford certain freedoms.
—Abbott Gleason

A really efficient totalitarian state would be one in which the
all-powerful executive of political bosses and their army of
managers control a population of slaves who do not have
to be coerced, because they love their servitude.
—Aldous Huxley

Whenever people start locking up enemies because
of national security without much legal care, you
are coming close [to fascism].
—Robert Paxton

For liberalism, the individual is the end, and society is the
means.... For fascism, society is the end, individuals
the means, and its whole life consists of using
individuals as instruments for its social ends.
—Alfredo Rocco

The best safeguard against fascism is to establish
social justice to the maximum extent possible.
—Arnold J. Toynbee

The liberty of a democracy is not safe if the people tolerate
the growth of private power to a point where it becomes
stronger than the democratic state itself. That in its essence
is fascism: ownership of government by an individual, by
a group, or any controlling private power.
—Franklin D. Roosevelt

FEAR

The only thing we really have to fear is fearmongering itself.
—Maureen Dowd

If people are good only because they fear punishment
and hope for reward, then we are a sorry lot indeed.
—Albert Einstein

We fear that we are inadequate, but our deepest fear
is that we are powerful beyond measure. It is our
light, not our darkness, that most frightens us.
—Marianne Williamson

You must do the thing you think you cannot do.
—Eleanor Roosevelt

The only thing we have to fear is fear itself.
—Franklin D. Roosevelt

I can't understand why people are frightened of
new ideas. I'm frightened of the old ones.
—John Cage

FEMINISM

I suppose I could have stayed home, baked cookies, and had teas, but what I decided was to fulfill my profession.
—Hillary Rodham Clinton

Psychotherapy—a long, drawn out process consisting of subtle probings of the human mind, whereby women are blamed for all of Freud's shortcomings.
—Marc Cooper

One distressing thing is the way men react to women who assert their equality: their ultimate weapon is to call them unfeminine. They think she is anti-male; they even whisper that she's probably a lesbian.
—Shirley Chisholm

Who knows what women can be when they are finally free to become themselves?
—Betty Friedan

Feminism is the radical notion that women are people.
—Cheris Kramarae and Paula Treichler

If I have to, I can do anything.
I am strong, I am invincible, I am woman.
—Helen Reddy

We hold these truths to be self-evident:
that all men and women are created equal.
—Elizabeth Cady Stanton

No man can call himself liberal, or radical, or even a conservative
advocate of fair play, if his work depends in any way on unpaid
or underpaid labor of women at home or in the office.
—Gloria Steinem

People call me a feminist whenever I express sentiments
that differentiate me from a doormat or a prostitute.
—Rebecca West

It's important to remember that feminism is no longer a group of
organizations or leaders. It's the expectations that parents have for
their daughters, and their sons, too. It's the way we talk about and
treat one another. It's who makes the money and who makes the
compromises and who makes the dinner.
—Anna Quindlen

FOOLS & FANATICS

Fervor is the weapon of choice of the impotent.
—Frantz Fanon

Wise men talk because they have something to
say; fools, because they have to say something.
—Plato

What is objectionable, what is dangerous, about extremists
is not that they are extreme, but that they are intolerant.
The evil is not what they say about their cause, but
what they say about their opponents.
—Robert F. Kennedy

There is no cosmic law forbidding the
triumph of extremism in America.
—Thomas McIntyre

The main doctrine of a fanatic's creed is
that his enemies are the enemies of God.
—Andrew White

The know-nothings are, unfortunately, seldom the do-nothings.
—Mignon McLaughlin

It is the property of fools, to be always judging.
—Thomas Fuller

Any fool can make a rule, and any fool will mind it.
—Henry David Thoreau

The best lack all conviction, while the
worst are full of passionate intensity.
—William Butler Yeats

FOREIGN POLICY

Human rights is the soul of our foreign policy, because
human rights is the very soul of our sense of nationhood.
—Jimmy Carter

In the United States today, the Declaration of Independence hangs
on schoolroom walls, but foreign policy follows Machiavelli.
—Howard Zinn

Shared risks, shared burdens, shared benefits—it's
not only a good motto for NATO, it's also a good
prescription for America's role in the world.
—Wesley Clark

Domestic policy can only lose elections.
Foreign policy can kill us all.
—John F. Kennedy

Think globally, act locally.
—Rene Dubos

There are very few wars that begin by design. Most war
begins as a result of miscalculation and accident and ratchet
intentions that people aren't smart enough to stop.
—Wesley Clark

The lack of objectivity, as far as foreign nations are
concerned, is notorious. From one day to another, another
nation is made out to be utterly depraved and fiendish,
while one's own nation stands for everything that is
good and noble.... Narcissistic distortion is the rule.
—Erich Fromm

America cannot and must not be the world's policeman.
We can't do everything. But we must do what we can do.
There are times and places where our leadership can
mean the difference between peace and war.
—Bill Clinton

FREEDOM

I call that mind free, which sets no bounds to its love,
which is not imprisoned in itself or in a sect, which
recognizes in all human beings the image of God.
—William Ellery Channing

He alone is worthy of life and freedom,
who each day does battle for them anew.
—Johann von Goethe

Freedom to differ is not limited to things that do not
matter much. That would be a mere shadow of freedom.
The test of its substance is the right to differ as to
things that touch the heart of the existing order.
—Robert Jackson

Life in freedom is not easy, and democracy is not perfect.
—John F. Kennedy

For to be free is not merely to cast off one's chains, but to live in a
way that respects and enhances the freedom of others.
—Nelson Mandela

Man is born free, and he is everywhere in chains.
—Jean-Jacques Rousseau

Man is condemned to be free.
—Jean-Paul Sartre

What our Constitution indispensably protects is the freedom
of each of us, be he Jew or agnostic, Christian or atheist,
Buddhist or freethinker, to believe or disbelieve, to worship
or not worship, to pray or keep silent, according to his own
conscience, uncoerced and unrestrained by government.
—Potter Stewart

Freethinkers are those who are willing to use their minds
without prejudice and without fearing to understand things
that clash with their own customs, privileges, or beliefs.
—Leo Tolstoy

FREE SPEECH

Unexpressed ideas, unpublished works,
unpurchased books are lost forever.
—American Library Association

The right to be heard does not automatically
include the right to be taken seriously.
—Hubert H. Humphrey

Free speech is about as good a cause
as the world has ever known.
—Heywood Broun

If we don't believe in freedom of expression for
people we despise, we don't believe in it at all.
—Noam Chomsky

Congress shall make no law respecting an establishment
of religion, or prohibiting the free exercise thereof; or
abridging the freedom of speech, or of the press, or the
right of the people peaceably to assemble; and to
petition the Government for a redress of grievances.
—First Amendment to the U.S. Constitution

One of the best ways to get yourself a reputation as a dangerous citizen these days is to go about repeating the very phrases which our founding fathers used in the struggle for independence.
—C. A. Beard

I disapprove of what you say, but I will defend to the death your right to say it.
—François Voltaire

The very aim of our institutions is just this: that we may think what we like and say what we think.
—Oliver Wendell Holmes

FUNDAMENTALISM

Fundamentalism is rigorously and systematically used to indoctrinate and subjugate young minds. It is a contraceptive designed to prevent intellectual fertilization.
—Stephen Jay Gould

The religious right is neither.
—Bumper sticker

Nobody is more dangerous than he who imagines himself pure in heart; for his purity, by definition, is unassailable.
—James Baldwin

The fundamentalist believer is mostly a weird intellectual who often lacks real faith altogether. As a self-appointed attorney for God…he very easily turns out to be more godless than the agnostic and the unbeliever.
—Steve Allen

But the greatest menace to our civilization today is the conflict between giant organized systems of self-righteousness— each system only too delighted to find that the other is wicked—each only too glad that the sins give it the pretext for still deeper hatred and animosity.
—Herbert Butterfield

My only enemy is right-wing religious fundamentalism.
—Bill Clinton

Islamic fundamentalism sounds disturbingly like Christian fundamentalism. They show the same instincts: damn the infidel, reverse modernity and scour the holy book for justification.
—Tom Enrich

Puritanism: The haunting fear that someone,
somewhere, may be happy.
—H. L. Mencken

Any movement that connects violence with God loses me, whether
it's the murder of a doctor at an abortion clinic or the murder of
busboys, firemen, or businessmen in the World Trade Center.
Radical fundamentalism at its core hates all the things I love.
—Tim Robbins

Fundamentalism isn't about religion, it's about power.
—Salman Rushdie

GAY & LESBIAN

No government has the right to tell its citizens when or whom to
love. The only queer people are those who don't love anybody.
—Rita Mae Brown

It's funny how heterosexuals have lives
and the rest of us have "lifestyles."
—Sonia Johnson

I think we ought to encourage stable family relationships, in whatever form they take. It just seems mean to deny gay couples in committed relationships any form of legal recognition.

—Suzanne Cassidy

All America loses if we let prejudice and discrimination stifle the hopes or deny the potential of a single American. All America loses when any person is denied or forced out of a job because of sexual orientation.

—Bill Clinton

From the time I was a kid, I have never been able to understand attacks upon the gay community. There are so many qualities that make up a human being...by the time I get through with all the things that I really admire about people, what they do with their private parts is probably so low on the list that it is irrelevant.

—Paul Newman

I've always felt that homophobic attitudes and policies were unjust and unworthy of a free society and must be opposed by all Americans who believe in democracy.

—Coretta Scott King

If homosexuality is a disease, let's all call in queer
to work. "Hello, can't work today, still queer."
—Robin Tyler

I finally got to a point where living honestly and being proud
of who I am was more important than fame. Ironically,
my being honest made me more famous.
—Ellen DeGeneres

Good parents are good parents, regardless of their sexual
orientation. It's clear that the sexual orientation of parents has
nothing to do with the sexual orientation of their children.
—Joycelyn Elders

The more people come out, the less it will be an issue.
If we are ashamed or ourselves, how the hell can we
expect the rest of the world not to be ashamed of us?
—Martina Navritilova

Keep the government out of my bedroom.
—Unknown

GOD AND GOD'S NATURE

If the concept of God has any validity or use, it can only
be to make us larger, freer, and more loving. If God
cannot do this, then it is time we got rid of him.
—James Balwin

Question with boldness even the existence of a God;
because, if there be one, he must more approve of the
homage of reason, than that of blindfolded fear.
—Thomas Jefferson

Who is the most famous liberal of all time? It simply
has to be God. No one is more generous, bounteous, or
misunderstood…. God's gift to us is beyond anything we
deserve or could possibly have expected, the gift of life.
—Forrester Church

Don't make me come down there.
—God

God has no religion.
—Mahatma Gandhi

I have too much respect for the idea of God to
make it responsible for such an absurd world.
—Georges Duhamel

I cannot imagine a God who rewards and punishes the objects of his
creation, whose purposes are modeled after our own—a God, in
short, who is but a reflection of human frailty. Neither can I believe
that the individual survives the death of his body, although feeble
minds harbor such thoughts through fear or ridiculous egotisms.
—Albert Einstein

Whatever there is of God and goodness in the universe,
it must work itself out and express itself through us.
—Albert Einstein

If God did not exist, it would be necessary to invent him.
—François Voltaire

I believe in God, only I spell it Nature.
—Frank Lloyd Wright

Is man one of God's blunders or is God one of man's blunders?
—Friedrich Nietzsche

God is not dead, but alive and well and
working on a much less ambitious project.
—Unknown

Either God wants to abolish evil, and cannot;
or he can, but does not want to.
—Epicurus

GOVERNMENT

There is something wrong in a government where they who
do the most have the least. There is something wrong when
honesty wears a rag, and rascality a robe; when the loving,
the tender, eat a crust, while the infamous sit at banquets.
—Robert Ingersoll

You can't say you love your country and hate your government.
—Bill Clinton

I am working for the time when unqualified blacks, browns, and
women join the unqualified men in running our government.
—Sissy Farenthold

The first duty of government is to protect
the powerless against the powerful.
—Code of Hammarabi

No man is good enough to govern another
man without that other's consent.
—Abraham Lincoln

Those who want the government to regulate matters of
the mind and spirit are like men who are so afraid
of being murdered that they commit suicide.
—Harry S. Truman

It is better to be governed well by sinners
than to be misgoverned by saints.
—Michael Lind

A society of sheep must in time beget a government of wolves.
—Henry de Jouvenel

Bureaucracy, the rule of no one, has
become the modern form of despotism.
—Mary McCarthy

Liberal institutions straightaway cease from being
liberal the moment they are soundly established.
—Friedrich Nietzsche

Let us never forget that government is
ourselves and not an alien power over us.
—Franklin D. Roosevelt

Government is the Entertainment Division
of the military-industrial complex.
—Frank Zappa

GREATNESS

The greatness of a nation is not the military power to
enforce its will upon others, but rather its capacity to
inspire high ideals and a humanizing spirit.
—James A. Forbes

Mediocrity knows nothing higher than itself;
but talent instantly recognizes genius.
—Sir Arthur Conan Doyle

It's time for greatness—not for greed. It's a time for
idealism—not ideology. It is a time not just for
compassionate words, but compassionate action.
—Marian Wright Edelman

It is not conquest that claims the warrior to be a hero, but the
goodness of his cause, and the use he makes of victory.
—Jane Porter

There is a melancholy that stems from greatness of mind.
—Sébastien Roch Nicolas Chamfort

I think this is the most extraordinary collection of talent, of
human knowledge [forty-nine Nobel Laureates], that has
ever been gathered at the White House—with the possible
exception of when Thomas Jefferson dined alone.
—John F. Kennedy

In every work of genius we recognize our own rejected thoughts.
—Ralph Waldo Emerson

There is no passion to be found playing small—in settling
for a life that is less than the one you are capable of living.
—Nelson Mandela

GREED

To have and not give is often worse than to steal.
—Marle von Ebner-Eschenbach

Fight the greedy and help the needy.
—Carol Moseley-Braun

There's enough on this planet for everyone's
needs, but not for everyone's greed.
—Mahatma Gandhi

You can't have everything. Where would you put it?
—Steven Wright

When we have provided against the cold, hunger,
and thirst, all the rest is but vanity and excess.
—Seneca

No crime is greater than approving of greed.
—Lao Tze

GREEN PARTY

We are building a democratic movement that will take this country
back from the corporate hooligans who have hijacked it from us.
—David Cobb

The only difference between the Republican and Democratic
parties is the velocities with which their knees hit the
floor when corporations knock on their door.
—Ralph Nader

We need an alternative for people who
believe in a fair and just society.
—Roy Williams

The Greens carry forward the traditional values of the Left:
freedom, equality, and solidarity. We want to create a truly
democratic society without class exploitation or social domination.
—Green Party Platform

GROWTH

Growth for the sake of growth is the ideology of the cancer cell.
—Edward Abbey

Life is a petty thing unless it is moved by the
indomitable urge to extend its boundaries.
—José Ortega y Gasset

One thing at a time, all things in succession.
That which grows slowly endures.
—J. G. Hubbard

A person can grow only as much as his horizon allows.
—John Powell

Everyone who knows how to read has it in their power to
magnify themselves, to multiply the ways in which they
exist, to make their life full, significant, and interesting.
—Aldous Huxley

The cure for boredom is curiosity. There is no cure for curiosity.
—Ellen Parr

GUNS

I am not anti-gun. I'm pro-knife. Consider the merits of the knife. In the first place, you have to catch up with someone in order to stab him. A general substitution of knives for guns would promote physical fitness. We'd turn into a whole nation of great runners. Plus, knives don't ricochet. And people are seldom killed while cleaning their knives.

—Molly Ivins

If you are the type of person who likes assault weapons, there is a place for you—the United States Army. We have them.

—Wesley Clark

More teenagers die of gunshot wounds than of all natural diseases combined.

—Center for Disease Control and Prevention

I believe everybody in the world should have guns. Citizens should have bazookas and rocket launchers too. I believe that all citizens should have their weapons of choice. However, I also believe that only I should have the ammunition.

—Scott Adams

The gun lobby finds waiting periods inconvenient. You have only to ask my husband how inconvenient he finds his wheelchair from time to time.

—Sarah Brady

I'm certainly in favor of all the gun control we can get—but if we want to rebuild our frayed civil society, we'd better reload young people's hearts and spirits at the same time.

—Arianna Huffington

HAPPINESS

Three grand essentials to happiness in this life are something to do, something to love, and something to hope for.

—Joseph Addison

Happiness consists not in having much, but in being content with little.

—Lady Marguerite Blessington

The only true happiness comes from squandering ourselves for a purpose.

—John Mason Brown

Happiness and the absurd are two sons of
the same earth. They are inseparable.
—Albert Camus

Happiness is when what you think, what you
say, and what you do are in harmony.
—Mahatma Gandhi

It is not easy to find happiness in ourselves,
and it is impossible to find it elsewhere.
—Agnes Repplier

People take different roads seeking fulfillment
and happiness. Just because they are not on
your road does not mean they have gotten lost.
—H. Jackson Brown, Jr.

He who is not contented with what he has, will
not be contented with what he doesn't have.
—Socrates

Happiness is not the absence of conflict,
but the ability to cope with it.
—Unknown

HATE

It is better to be hated for what you are
than loved for what you are not.
—André Gide

A man who lives not by what he loves
but what he hates is a sick man.
—Archibald MacLeish

In hatred, as in love, we grow like the thing we brood upon.
—Mary Renault

Take care that no one hates you justly.
—Publilius Syrus

I will permit no man to narrow and degrade
my soul by making me hate him.
—Booker T. Washington

If you hate a person, you hate something in him that is part of
yourself. What isn't part of ourselves doesn't disturb us.
—Hermann Hesse

You cannot hate other people without hating yourself.
—Oprah Winfrey

HOPE

To eat bread without hope is still slowly to starve to death.
—Pearl S. Buck

The road that is built in hope is more pleasant to the
traveler than the road built in despair, even though
they both lead to the same destination.
—Marian Zimmer Bradley

To live without hope is to cease to live.
—Fyodor Dostoevsky

We should not let our fears hold us back from pursuing our hopes.
—John F. Kennedy

Hope is a good thing, maybe the best of
things, and no good thing ever dies.
—Stephen King

HUMANISM

I cannot affirm God if I fail to affirm man.
—Norman Cousins

In the end, anti-black, anti-female, and all forms of discrimination
are equivalent to the same thing—anti-humanism.
—Shirley Chisholm

A humanist has four leading characteristics—curiosity, a free
mind, belief in good taste, and belief in the human race.
—E. M. Forster

No deity will save us; we must save ourselves.
—Paul Kurtz

I retain my belief in the nobility and excellence in
the human. I believe that spiritual sweetness and
unselfishness will conquer the gross gluttony of today.
—Jack London

We have lost religion, but we have found humanism.
—Jean-Paul Sartre

We are becoming the servants in thought, as in action,
of the machine we have created to serve us.
—John Kenneth Galbraith

I am a Humanist, which means, in part, that I have
tried to behave decently without expectations of
rewards or punishment after I am dead.
—Kurt Vonnegut

Humanism is the creed of those who believe that in the circle of
enwrapping mystery, men's fates are in their own hands, a faith
that for modern man is becoming the only possible fate.
—John Galsworthy

THE HUMAN CONDITION

We are all in the same boat, in a stormy sea,
and we owe each other a terrible loyalty.
—G. K. Chesterton

If you smile at me I will understand, because that is something
everybody, everywhere does in the same language.
—David Crosby

Everything is held together with stories. That is all that is holding
us together, stories and compassion.

—Barry Lopez

It's a fool who plays it cool by making this world a little colder.

—Paul McCartney and John Lennon

Our problems are man-made, therefore they may be solved by
man.... No problem of human destiny is beyond human beings.

—John F. Kennedy

It is an ironic habit of human beings to run
faster when we have lost our way.

—Rollo May

HUMAN NATURE

Man is by nature good; men are depraved and perverted by society.

—Jean-Jacques Rousseau

No man is an island, entire of itself; every man
is a part of the continent, a part of the main.

—John Donne

What the scientific study of human motives shows is that human nature is neither essentially bad nor essentially good…. But human nature is essentially flexible and educable.

—Corliss Lamont

In man, creature and creator are united.

—Friedrich Nietzsche

The veil between us and the divine is more permeable than we imagine.

—Sue Patton Thoele

HUMAN RIGHTS

Freedom is never voluntarily given by the oppressor; it must be demanded by the oppressed.

—Martin Luther King, Jr.

My concept of human rights has grown to include not only the rights to live in peace, but also to adequate health care, shelter, food, and to economic opportunity.

—Jimmy Carter

A human being is not to be handled as
a tool, but is to respected and revered.
—Felix Adler

Developing countries may have slightly different concepts of
human rights than the West, but it is not cultural imperialism
to suggest that women should not be mutilated, enslaved,
or condemned to die in childbirth.
—Renee Loth

The future belongs to those who believe
in the beauty of their dreams.
—Eleanor Roosevelt

Most people, no doubt, when they espouse human
rights, make their own mental reservations about
the proper application of the word "human."
—Suzanne LaFollette

Human rights rest on human dignity. The dignity of
man is an ideal worth fighting for and worth dying for.
—Robert Maynard

IDEALISM

Our ideals are our better selves.
—Amos Bronson Alcott

Most of the things worth doing in the world have been declared impossible before they were done.
—Louis Brandeis

The discrepancy between American ideals and American practice creates a dry rot which eats away at the foundations of our democratic faith.
—Helen Gahagan Douglas

I keep my ideals, because in spite of everything I still believe that people are really good at heart.
—Anne Frank

The problems of the world cannot possibly be solved by skeptics or cynics whose horizons are limited by the obvious realities. We need men who can dream of things that never were.
—John F. Kennedy

Each time a man stands up for an ideal or acts to improve the lot of others or strikes out against injustice, he sends forth a tiny ripple of hope, and crossing each other from a million different centers of energy and daring, those ripples build a current that can sweep down the mightiest walls of oppression and resistance.
—Robert F. Kennedy

Some men see things the way they are and ask "Why?" I see things the way they might be and ask "Why not?"
—George Bernard Shaw

Idealists are people who believe in the potential of human nature for transformation.... It is always within our power to change our nature.
—M. Scott Peck

Shifting society's discourse from one of selfishness and cynicism to one of idealism and caring is the first and most important political goal...in the next several decades.
—Michael Lerner

Go confidently in the direction of your dreams. Live the life you have imagined.
—Henry David Thoreau

INDEPENDENCE

There will never be a really free and enlightened state until the state comes to recognize the individual as a higher and independent power, from which all its own power and authority are derived.
—Henry David Thoreau

Independence I have long considered as the grand blessing of life, the basis of every virtue.
—Mary Wollstonecraft

I am a sect by myself, as far as I know.
—Thomas Jefferson

Self-reliance is the only road to true freedom, and being one's own person is its ultimate reward.
—Patricia Sampson

The most powerful single force in the world today is neither communism nor capitalism, neither the H-bomb nor the guided missile—it is man's eternal desire to be free and independent.
—John F. Kennedy

Whoso goes to walk alone, accuses the whole world; he declareth all to be unfit to be his companions; it is very uncivil, nay, insulting; Society will retaliate.
—Ralph Waldo Emerson

INDIVIDUALITY

No man should part with his individuality to become another. No process is so fatal as that which would cast all men into one mould.
—William Ellery Channing

There is something different about democratic individuality which is very different from rugged, ragged, rapacious individuality.
—Cornell West

If fifty million people say a foolish thing, it is still a foolish thing.
—Anatole France

The shoe that fits one person pinches another; there is no recipe for living that suits all cases.
—Carl G. Jung

To be nobody but yourself in a world which is doing its best, night and day, to make you like everybody else means to fight the hardest battle any human being can fight; and never stop fighting.
—E. E. Cummings

Every man is his own Pygmalion, and spends his life fashioning himself. And in fashioning himself, for good or ill, he fashions the human race and its future.
—I. F. Stone

The individual has always had to struggle to keep from being overwhelmed by the tribe. To be your own man is a hard business. If you try it, you will be lonely often, and sometimes frightened. But no price is too high to pay for the privilege of owning yourself.
—Rudyard Kipling

INFERIORITY

The greater the feeling of inferiority that has been experienced, the more powerful is the urge to conquest and the more violent the emotional agitation.
—Alfred Adler

I am the inferior of any man whose rights I trample under foot.
—Robert Ingersoll

No one can make you feel inferior without your consent.
—Eleanor Roosevelt

An inferiority complex would be a blessing,
if only the right people had it.
—Alan Reed

The inability to act spontaneously, to express what one genuinely feels and thinks, and the resulting necessity to present a pseudo-self to others and oneself, are the root of the feeling of inferiority.
—Erich Fromm

INNER LIFE

The outward freedom that we shall attain will only be in exact proportion to the inward freedom to which we may have grown at a given moment. And if this is a correct view of freedom, our chief energy must be concentrated on achieving reform from within.
—Mahatma Gandhi

The greatest revolution of our generation is the discovery that human beings, by changing the inner attitudes of their minds, can change the outer aspects of their lives.
—William James

What happens to a man is less significant
than what happens within him.
—Louis L. Mann

Most true happiness comes from one's inner life, from the disposition of the mind and soul. Admittedly, a good inner life is hard to achieve, especially in these trying times. It takes reflection and contemplation and self-discipline.
—William L. Shirer

To persevere is always a reflection of the state of one's inner life, one's philosophy, and one's perspective.
—David Guterson

If we could read the secret history of our enemies, we should find in each man's life sorrow and suffering enough to disarm all hostility.
—Henry Wadsworth Longfellow

In everyone's life, at some time, our inner fire goes
out. It is then burst into flame by an encounter with
another human being. We should all be thankful
for those people who rekindle the inner spirit.
—Albert Schweitzer

INSANITY

Insanity is doing the same thing over and
over again, but expecting different results.
—Albert Einstein

The only people for me are the mad ones. The ones who are mad
to love, mad to talk, mad to be saved; the ones who never yawn or
say a commonplace thing, but burn, burn, burn like fabulous yellow
Roman candles exploding like spiders across the stars.
—Jack Kerouac

Madness need not be all breakdown. It may also be
breakthrough. It is potential liberation and renewal,
as well as enslavement and existential death.
—R. D. Laing

Insanity in individuals is something rare—but in
groups, parties, nations and epochs, it is the rule.
—Friedrich Nietzsche

In every society, the definitions of sanity and
madness are arbitrary—are, in a sense, political.
—Susan Sontag

You're only given a little spark of madness. You mustn't lose it.
—Robin Williams

Man's sensitivity to little things and insensitivity to
the greatest are the signs of a strange disorder.
—Blaise Pascal

INSPIRATION

Don't loaf and invite inspiration. Light out after it with a club.
—Jack London

Inspiration usually comes during work, rather than before it.
—Madeleine L'Engle

Inspirations never go in for long engagements;
they demand immediate marriage to action.
—Brendan Francis

As I grow older, part of my emotional survival plan must be to
actively seek inspiration instead of passively waiting for it to find me.
—Bebe Moore Campbell

An age is called Dark not because the light fails
to shine, but because people refuse to see it.
—James Michener

We have always held to the hope, the belief, the conviction that
there is a better life, a better world, beyond the horizon.
—Franklin D. Roosevelt

INTEGRITY

Nothing so completely baffles one who is full of trick and duplicity
himself, than straightforward and simple integrity in another.
—Charles Caleb Colton

A man in a corrupted age must make a secret of his integrity,
or else he will be looked upon as a common enemy.
—Marquis of Halifax

Integrity simply means a willingness not to violate one's identity.
—Erich Fromm

This old anvil laughs at many broken hammers.
There are men who can't be bought.
—Carl Sandburg

Never separate the lives you live from the words you speak.
—Paul Wellstone

Be loyal to people in their absence.
—Stephen Covey

INTELLECTUALS

It is the responsibility of intellectuals
to speak the truth and expose lies.
—Noam Chomsky

There's always something suspect about
an intellectual on the winning side.
—Vaclav Havel

The way of the egghead is hard.
—Adlai Stevenson

Practical men, who believe themselves to be quite exempt
from any intellectual influences, are usually the slaves of
some defunct economist. Madmen in authority, who hear
voices in the air, are distilling their frenzy from some
academic scribbler of a few years back.
—John Maynard Keynes

The decision to speak out is the vocation and
life-long peril by which the intellectual must live.
—Kay Boyle

INTELLIGENCE

American political opportunities are loaded against
those who are simultaneously intelligent and honest.
—Richard Dawkins

Intelligence, yes, but of what kind and aim? There is the intelligence
of Socrates and the intelligence of the thief or a forger.
—Ralph Waldo Emerson

Everyone is entitled to his own opinion, but not his own facts.
—Daniel Patrick Moynihan

Everybody is ignorant, only on different subjects.
—Will Rogers

Do not judge my intelligence by the answers
I give, but instead by the questions I ask.
—Mark McGranaghan

INTUITION

It is through science that we prove,
but through intuition that we discover.
—Henri Poincare

Intuition is not contrary to reason,
but outside the province of reason.
—Carl G. Jung

The intuitive mind is a sacred gift and the rational mind is a faithful servant. We have created a society that honors the servant and has forgotten the gift.

—Albert Einstein

Intuition is a spiritual faculty and does not explain, but simply points the way.

—Florence Scovel Shinn

Trust yourself. You know more than you think you do.

—Benjamin Spock

IRAQ WAR

Today I weep for my country.... Around the globe, our friends mistrust us, our word is disputed, our intentions are questioned.

—Robert Byrd

As soon as one nation claims the right to take preventive action, other countries will naturally do the same. If we go down that road, where are we going?

— Jacques Chirac

I think the whole policy of pre-emptive
war is a serious, serious mistake.
—Walter Cronkite

This [Iraq] war could go on forever, no matter how unpopular it
gets. That's very like Vietnam: a stale, hopeless occupation.
—Daniel Ellsberg

The White House wants to paint the picture in Iraq as rosy, so the
Pentagon has banned photos of coffins and body bags leaving Iraq or
arriving in the United States. Worse, the president hasn't attended
funerals or memorials for the soldiers who have lost their lives.
—Jesse Jackson

The American people were told Saddam Hussein was building
nuclear weapons. He was not. We were told he had stockpiles
of other weapons of mass destruction. He did not. We were
told he was involved in 9/11. He was not. We were told Iraq was
attracting terrorists from Al Qaeda. It was not. We were told our
soldiers would be viewed as liberators. They are not. We were
told Iraq could pay for its own reconstruction. It cannot. We
were told the war would make America safer. It has not.
—Ted Kennedy

We have made enemies of one billion Muslims.
—Gore Vidal

The USA is a threat to world peace. Who are they to pretend that they are the policemen of the world, the ones that should decide for the people of Iraq what should be done with their government and their leadership. All that [the USA] wants is Iraqi oil.
—Nelson Mandela

America has taken a country that was not
a terrorist threat and turned it into one.
—Jessica Stern

The lie that brought us into war was that Iraq was a threat to us.... It was an attempt at a corporate takeover. This was about oil. It wasn't about human rights.
—Janeane Garofalo

How Bush and his junta succeeded in deflecting America's anger from bin Laden to Saddam Hussein is one of the great public relations conjuring tricks in history.
—John Le Carre

Bush's policy of pre-emptive war is immoral—
such a policy would legitimize Pearl Harbor.
—Helen Thomas

We live in fictitious times. We live in the time where
we have fictitious election results that elects a fictitious
president. We live in a time where we have a man sending
us to war for fictitious reasons…We are against this war,
Mr. Bush. Shame on you, Mr. Bush. Shame on you.
—Michael Moore

JESUS CHRIST

Jesus was a liberal.
—Bumper sticker

Jesus preached and talked against a whole gamut
of sins. He never mentioned homosexuality at all.
—Jimmy Carter

Jesus was the first socialist, the first
to seek a better life for mankind.
—Mikhail Gorbachev

Did Jesus spend his life hobnobbing or schmoozing
with the powerful, or did he spend his life in
solidarity and relationship with the poor?
—Matt Zemek

JUSTICE

When the man who feeds the world by toiling in the fields is
himself deprived of the basic rights of feeding, sheltering, and
caring for his own family, the whole community of man is sick.
—Cesar Chavez

Charity begins at home and justice begins next door.
—Charles Dickens

An injustice is tolerable only when it is necessary
to avoid an even greater injustice.
—John Rawls

The answer to injustice is not to silence
the critic, but to end the injustice.
—Paul Robeson

Military justice is to justice what military music is to music.
—Groucho Marx

A society that has more justice is a society that needs less charity.
—Ralph Nader

Don't let the politicians chip away at the New Deal and
the Great Society programs like Social Security, Medicare,
that puts a floor beyond which the elderly, the sick, the
powerless do not starve or lack for medicine or shelter.
—Helen Thomas

Injustice anywhere is a threat to justice everywhere.
—Martin Luther King, Jr.

Be ashamed to die till you have won some victory for humanity.
—Horace Mann

KINDNESS

No act of kindness, however small, is ever wasted.
—Aesop

This is my simple religion. There is no need for temples; no need for complicated philosophy. Our own brain, our own heart is our temple; the philosophy is kindness.
—Dalai Lama

You cannot do a kindness too soon, for you never know when it will be too late.
—Ralph Waldo Emerson

I expect to pass through this world but once, therefore any good that I can do, or any kindness that I can show to any fellow creature, let me do it now; let me not defer it or neglect it, for I shall not pass this way again.
—Stephen Grellet

Three things in human life are important. The first is to be kind. The second is to be kind. And the third is to be kind.
—Henry James

Praise out of season, or tactlessly bestowed, can freeze the heart as much as blame.
—Pearl S. Buck

LABOR UNIONS

The Labor Movement: the people who brought you the weekend.
—Bumper sticker

Every advance in this half-century—Social Security, civil
rights, Medicare, aid to education, one after another—
came with the support and leadership of American Labor.
—Jimmy Carter

We must all hang together, or most
assuredly, we shall all hang separately.
—Benjamin Franklin

What does labor want?… We want more schoolhouses and less
jails; more books and less arsenals; more learning and less vice;
more leisure and less greed; more justice and less revenge.
—Samuel Gompers

It is one of the characteristics of a free and democratic
nation that it have free and independent labor unions.
—Franklin D. Roosevelt

The labor movement means just this: It is the last noble protest of the American people against the power of incorporated wealth.
—Wendell Phillips

LAWS

The less people know about how sausages and laws are made, the better they'll sleep at night.
—Otto von Bismarck

The law, in its majestic equality, forbids rich and poor alike to sleep under bridges, beg in the streets, or steal bread.
—Anatole France

An unjust law is itself a species of violence. Arrest for its breach is more so.
—Mahatma Gandhi

Morality cannot be legislated, but behavior can be regulated. Judicial decrees may not change the heart, but they can restrain the heartless.
—Martin Luther King, Jr.

Good people do not need laws to tell them to act responsibly,
while bad people will find a way around the laws.
—Plato

It is the spirit and not the form of the law that keeps justice alive.
—Earl Warren

Laws will not eliminate prejudice from the hearts of
human beings. But that is no reason to allow
prejudice to continue to be enshrined in our laws.
—Shirley Chisholm

LEADERSHIP

A leader is best when people barely know that he
exists…. When his work is done, his aim fulfilled,
they will all say, "We did this ourselves."
—Lao Tzu

There are two ways of spreading light: to
be the candle or the mirror that reflects it.
—Edith Wharton

Stories are the single most powerful tool in a leader's toolkit.
—Howard Gardner

Great leaders reinforce the idea that accomplishment in our society comes from great individual acts. We credit individuals for outcomes that required teams and communities to accomplish.
—Peter Block

Leaders don't create followers, they create more leaders.
—Tom Peters

If your actions inspire others to dream more, learn more, do more, and become more, you are a leader.
—John Quincy Adams

A leader takes people where they want to go. A great leader takes people where they don't necessarily want to go, but ought to be.
—Rosalynn Carter

Setting an example is not the main means of influencing others, it is the only means.
—Albert Einstein

Leaders are people we as followers want to regard with
awe as the fullest flowering of our own possibilities.
—Gail Sheehy

When trouble arises and things look bad, there is always
one individual who perceives a solution and is willing to
take command. Very often, that individual is crazy.
—Dave Barry

LEARNING

We learn more by looking for the answer to a question and not
finding it than we do from learning the answer itself.
—Lloyd Alexander

It is possible to store the mind with a million
facts and still be entirely uneducated.
—Alec Bourne

A liberal education frees a man from the prison-house of his
class, race, time, place, background, family, and even nation.
—Robert Maynard Hutchins

Of all the civil rights for which the world has struggled
and fought for five thousand years, the right to learn
is undoubtedly the most fundamental.
—W. E. B. DuBois

Hopefully, your education left much to be desired.
—Alan Greg

We learn to do something by doing it. There is no other way.
—John Holt

I don't know who I am. But life is for learning.
—Joni Mitchell

Every act of conscious learning requires the willingness to suffer
injury to one's self-esteem. That is why young children, before they
are aware of their self-importance, learn so easily; and why older
persons, especially if vain or important, cannot learn at all.
—Thomas Szasz

Education…has produced a vast population able to
read but unable to distinguish what is worth reading.
—G. M. Trevelyan

LIBERALISM

Known more for its fractiousness than its coherence, more for its mutability than its doctrinal consistency, liberalism is best defined as a state of mind: an attitude toward the possibilities of politics and culture that is both defiantly hopeful and deeply skeptical.

—Dorothy Wickenden

Of all the varieties of virtues, liberalism is the most beloved.

—Aristotle

Liberalism is not a fixed set of doctrines but a temper, a public spirit of openness and generosity.

—Forrester Church

Liberalism is trust of the people tempered by prudence. Conservatism is distrust of the people tempered by fear.

—William E. Gladstone

Liberalism…is the right which the majority concedes to minorities and hence it is the noblest cry that has ever resounded on this planet.

—José Ortega y Gasset

Liberalism…has learned ever more artfully to unite a constant protest against the government with a constant submission to it.
—**Alexander Herzen**

Liberalism, above all, means emancipation—
emancipation from one's fears, his inadequacies,
from prejudice, from discrimination…from poverty.
—**Hubert H. Humphrey**

There are two kinds of liberalism. A liberalism which is always, subterraneously authoritative and paternalistic, on the side of one's good conscience. And then there is a liberalism which is more ethical than political; one would have to find another name for this. Something like a profound suspension of judgment.
—**Roland Barthes**

LIBERALS

A liberal is a man or a woman or a child who looks forward to a better day, a more tranquil night, and a bright, infinite future.
—**Leonard Bernstein**

Liberals support the idea that individuals are more important than corporations, that as long as there are welfare programs for corporations there should be welfare programs for individuals.
—Jon Carroll

It's about time that liberals stood up proudly, declared that their views are deeply steeped in fine American tradition, and stopped running away from what they are.
—Alan Colmes

My faith has been the driving thing of my life. I think it is important that people who are perceived as liberals not be afraid of talking about moral and community values.
—Marian Wright Edelman

What passes for radical left-wing opinion in America today would fit comfortably into the platform of any center-right party in Europe.
—Phil Freeman

If your workplace is safe; if your children go to school rather than being forced into labor; if you are paid a living wage, including overtime; if you enjoy a forty-hour week and you are allowed to join a union to protect your rights; if your food is not poisoned and your water is drinkable; if your parents are eligible for

Medicare and Social Security, so they can grow old in dignity without bankrupting your family; if our rivers are getting cleaner and our air isn't black with pollution; if our wilderness is protected and our countryside is still green; if people of all races can share the same public facilities; if everyone has the right to vote; if couples fall in love and marry regardless of race; if we have finally begun to transcend a segregated society—you can thank liberals.

—Joe Conason

The liberal soul shall be made fat: and he that watereth shall be watered also himself.

—Proverbs 11:25

Somehow liberals have been unable to acquire from life what conservatives seem to be endowed with at birth: namely, a healthy skepticism of the powers of government agencies to do good.

—Daniel Moynihan

A liberal to me is someone who…is unbeholden to any specific belief or party or group or person, but makes up his or her mind on the basis of the facts.

—Walter Cronkite

Liberals feel unworthy of their possessions. Conservatives
feel they deserve everything they've stolen.

—Mort Sahl

A liberal is a man too broadminded
to take his own side in a quarrel.

—Robert Frost

Liberals have more questions than answers;
conservatives have more answers than questions.

—Unknown

The liberal holds that he is true to the
republic when he is true to himself.

—E. B. White

LIBERTY

Liberty is the possibility of doubting, the possibility of making a
mistake, the possibility of searching and experimenting, the
possibility of saying no to any authority—literary, artistic,
philosophic, religious, social, and even political.

—Ignazio Silone

America is not Rome. We do not dream
of empire. We dream of liberty for all.
—Howard Dean

The cost of liberty is less than the price of repression.
—W. E. B. DuBois

Those who would give up essential liberty to purchase a
little temporary safety, deserve neither liberty nor safety.
—Benjamin Franklin

The love of liberty is the love of others; the
love of power is the love of ourselves.
—William Hazlitt

Liberty without learning is always in peril;
learning without liberty is always in vain.
—John F. Kennedy

When liberty is taken away by force, it can be restored by force.
When it is relinquished by default it can never be recovered.
—Dorothy Thompson

Give me liberty or give me death.
—Patrick Henry

LIFE

I don't want to get to the end of my life and find that I have lived
just the length of it. I want to have lived the width of it, as well.
—Diane Ackerman

Life is full of misery, loneliness, and
suffering—and it's all over much too soon.
—Woody Allen

Do every act of your life as if it were your last.
—Marcus Aurelius

The chief event of life is the day in which we
have encountered a mind that startled us.
—Ralph Waldo Emerson

Life is the sum of your choices.
—Albert Camus

I am convinced that the world is not a mere bog in which men and women trample themselves in the mire and die. Something magnificent is taking place here amid the cruelties and tragedies.
—Charles Beard

Live as if you were to die tomorrow.
Learn as if you were to live forever.
—Mahatma Gandhi

Dost thou love life? Then do not squander time, for that is the stuff life is made of.
—Benjamin Franklin

Our lives begin to end the day we become silent about things that matter.
—Martin Luther King, Jr.

Life isn't about finding yourself. Life is about creating yourself.
—George Bernard Shaw

These, then, are my last words to you: Be not afraid of life. Believe that life is worth living, and your belief will help create that fact.
—William James

The mass of men lead lives of quiet desperation. A stereotyped
but unconscious despair is concealed even under what
are called the games and amusements of mankind.
—Henry David Thoreau

Men go fishing all of their lives without
knowing that it is not fish they are after.
—Henry David Thoreau

If you haven't found something strange
during the day, it hasn't been much of a day.
—John A. Wheeler

The unexamined life is not worth living.
—Socrates

Many people reach their conclusions about life like lazy school
children. They copy the answers from the back of the book
without troubling to work out the sum for themselves.
—Søren Kierkegaard

A bird doesn't sing because it has an answer,
it sings because it has a song.
—Maya Angelou

LOVE

Love elevates or degrades; it never permits us to remain ourselves.
—Gustave Le Bon

We are shaped and guided by what we love.
—Johann von Goethe

Love is an act of sedition, a revolt against reason,
an uprising in the body politic, a private mutiny.
—Diane Ackerman

Love is patient; love is kind; love is not envious or boastful or
arrogant or rude. It does not insist on its own way; it is not
irritable or resentful; it does not rejoice in wrongdoing, but
rejoices in the truth. It bears all things, believes all things,
hopes all things, endures all things. Love never ends.
—1 Corinthians 13:4–7

I believe our concept of romantic love is irrational, impossible
to fulfill, and the cause of many broken homes. No human
being can maintain that rarefied atmosphere of "true love."
—Rita Mae Brown

Love is the condition in which the happiness
of another person is essential to your own.
—Robert Heinlein

Do you want me to tell you something really subversive?
Love is everything it's cracked up to be. It really is worth
fighting for, being brave for, risking everything for.
—Erica Jong

Love doesn't just sit there, like a stone; it has to be
made, like bread, remade all the time, made new.
—Ursula K. Le Guin

Love is the extremely difficult realization
that someone other than oneself is real.
—Iris Murdoch

I believe that we are called to stand on the side of love.
Love strains to know the other, not shut the other out.
—William Sinkford

I thought that if I could only see one person
for all eternity, I would want it to be you.
—Marianne Martin

MARRIAGE

Marriage probably originated as a straightforward food-for-sex deal among foraging primates. Compatibility was not a big issue, nor, of course, was there any tension over who would control the remote.

—Barbara Ehrenreich

I learnt a long time ago that the only two people who count in any marriage are the two that are in it.

—Hillary Rodham Clinton

A successful marriage requires falling in love many times, always with the same person.

—Mignon McLaughlin

Success in marriage does not come merely through finding the right mate, but through being the right mate.

—Barnett Brickner

Marriages don't last. When I meet a guy, the first question I ask myself is: "Is this the man I want my children to spend their weekends with?"

—Rita Rudner

Marry the right person. This one decision will
determine 90 percent of your happiness or misery.
—H. Jackson Brown, Jr.

If divorce has increased by one thousand percent, don't
blame the women's movement. Blame the obsolete
sex roles on which our marriages were based.
—Betty Friedan

Getting married is the boldest and most
idealistic thing that most of us will ever do.
—Maggie Gallagher

I was married by a judge. I should have asked for a jury.
—Groucho Marx

People should not be discriminated against in the
exercise of their civil rights, and the right to marry
who you want to marry is one of those rights.
—Carol Moseley-Braun

I married beneath me, all women do.
—Nancy Astor

Gay and lesbian couples who want to wed aren't trying to
assail the grounds for marriage. They're trying to share them.
—Ellen Goodman

I have yet to hear a man ask for advice
on how to combine marriage and a career.
—Gloria Steinem

MATERIALISM

He will always be a slave who does
not know how to live upon a little.
—Horace

Our economic system must create men who fit its needs; men who
cooperate smoothly; men who want to consume more and more.
—Erich Fromm

My primary concern is that we over-invest
in things and under-invest in people.
—John Kenneth Galbraith

I was part of that strange race of people aptly described as spending their lives doing things they detest to make money they don't want to buy things they don't need to impress people they dislike.
—Emile Henry Gauvreay

Too many of us now tend to worship self-indulgence and consumption. Human identity is no longer defined by what one does, but by what one owns.
—Jimmy Carter

This focus on money and power may do wonders in the marketplace, but it creates a tremendous crisis in our society. People who have spent all day learning how to sell themselves and to manipulate others are in no position to form lasting friendships or intimate relationships.
—Michael Lerner

A man is rich in proportion to the number of things which he can afford to let alone.
—Henry David Thoreau

A society in which consumption has to be artificially stimulated in order to keep production going is society founded on trash and waste.
—Dorothy L. Sayers

MCCARTHYISM

McCarthyism: 1. The practice of publicizing accusations of political disloyalty or subversion with insufficient regard to evidence. 2. The use of unfair investigatory or accusatory methods in order to suppress opposition.
—*American Heritage Dictionary*

No one can terrorize a whole nation, unless we are all his accomplices.
—Edward R. Murrow

The term "terrorism" is taking on the same kind of characteristics as the term "communism" did in the 1950s. It stops people in their tracks, and they're willing to give up their freedoms…and to scapegoat people, especially immigrants and people who criticize the war.
—Nadine Strossen

When public men indulge themselves in abuse, when they deny others a fair trial, when they resort to innuendo and insinuation, to libel, scandal, and suspicion, then our democratic society is outraged, and democracy is baffled. It has no apparatus to deal with the boor, the liar, the lout, and the antidemocrat in general.
—J. William Fulbright

MEANING

The meaning of things lies not in the things themselves, but in our attitude towards them.
—Antoine de Saint-Exupery

Life may have no meaning. Or even worse, it may have a meaning of which I disapprove.
—Ashleigh Brilliant

What man actually needs is not a tensionless state, but rather the striving and struggling for some goal worthy of him. What he needs is not the discharge of tension at any cost, but the call of a potential meaning waiting to be fulfilled by him.
—Victor Frankl

There is no meaning in life except the meaning
man gives his life by unfolding his powers.
—Erich Fromm

If logic tells you that life is a meaningless
accident, don't give up on life. Give up on logic.
—Shira Milgrom

There is a place where we are always alone
with our own mortality, where we must have
something greater than ourselves to hold onto.
—Dorothy Allison

MEDIA

What journalism is really about; it's to
monitor power and the centers of power.
—Amira Hass

The media in the wealthy world are becoming increasingly
simplistic, superficial, and celebrity-focused.
—Laurie Garrett

Conservatives enjoy their virtual monopoly over the
nation's political conversation…. They paid a lot
of money for it and they intend to keep it.
—Joe Conason

The professed concern for freedom of the press in the West is
not very persuasive in the light of…the actual performance
of the media in serving the powerful and privileged as an
agency of manipulation, indoctrination, and control.
—Noam Chomsky

Remember the old joke about politics being show
business for ugly people? Well, right-wing radio is
niche entertainment for the spiritually unattractive.
—Hendrik Hertzberg

The Founders didn't count on the rise of mega-media. They
didn't count on huge private corporations that would own
not only the means of journalism but also vast swaths
of the territory that journalism should be covering.
—Bill Moyers

In America, the arms industry, the oil industry, the major
media networks, and, indeed, U.S. foreign policy, are
all controlled by the same business combines.
—Arundhati Roy

Americans are the best entertained and
the least informed people in the world.
—Neil Postman

Trying to determine what is going on in the world
by reading newspapers is like trying to tell the
time by watching the second hand of a clock.
—Ben Hecht

If you're not careful the media will have you hating
the people who are being oppressed, and loving
the people who are doing the oppressing.
—Malcolm X

Modern politics today requires a mastery of television.
I've never really warmed up to television and, in
fairness to television, it's never warmed up to me.
—Walter F. Mondale

News is what someone, somewhere is trying
to suppress, the rest is just advertising.
—Lord Northcliffe

A liberal bias? I don't know what a liberal bias is. Do you
mean we care about the poor, the sick, and the maimed?
Do we care whether people are being shot every day
on the streets of America? If that's liberal, so be it.
—Helen Thomas

Journalism is in drastic decline…. The commercial media are
greed-driven enterprises dominated by a dozen transnational
companies. Newsroom staffs have been downsized. Much
of what you see on national and local TV news is actually
video news releases prepared by public-relations firms
and given free to TV stations and networks.
—John Stauber

If those in charge of our society—politicians, corporate executives,
and owners of press and television—can dominate our ideas,
they will be secure in their power. They will not need soldiers
patrolling the streets. We will control ourselves.
—Howard Zinn

MODERATION

The hottest places in hell are reserved for those who, in time of great moral crises, maintain their neutrality.

—Dante

Extreme positions are not succeeded by moderate ones, but by contrary extreme positions.

—Friedrich Nietzsche

I have almost reached the regrettable conclusion that the Negro's great stumbling block in his stride toward freedom is not the White Citizen's Councilor or the Ku Klux Klanner, but the white moderate.

—Martin Luther King, Jr.

Compromise makes a good umbrella, but a poor roof; it is a temporary expedient, often wise in party politics, almost sure to be unwise in statesmanship.

—James Russell Lowell

I want to stay as close to the edge as I can without going over. Out on the edge you see all kinds of things you can't see from the center.

—Kurt Vonnegut

Political liberty is to be found only in moderate governments.
—Charles de Montesquieu

Moderation in temper is always a virtue;
but moderation in principle is always a vice.
—Thomas Paine

Let him know how to choose the mean and avoid the extremes on
either side, as far as possible. For this is the way of happiness.
—Plato

Every reasonable human being should be a moderate socialist.
—Thomas Mann

MORALITY

My experience had been that the people who talk the loudest
about morality are the people who possess the least amount of it.
—James Carville

Never let your sense of morals keep you from doing what is right.
—Isaac Asimov

Waste no more time arguing what a good man should be. Be one.
—Marcus Aurelius

The greatest tragedy in mankind's entire history
may be the hijacking of morality by religion.
—Arthur C. Clarke

The Golden Rule is of no use whatsoever
unless you realize that it is your move.
—Frank Crane

There is nothing divine about morality, it is a purely human affair.
—Albert Einstein

Respect for the truth comes close
to being the basis for all morality.
—Frank Herbert

The true measure of a man is how he treats
someone who can do him absolutely no good.
—Samuel Johnson

I was raised the old-fashioned way, with a stern
set of moral principles: Never lie, cheat, steal,
or knowingly spread a venereal disease.
—Barbara Ehrenreich

The problem with people who have no vices
is that generally you can be pretty sure they're
going to have some pretty annoying virtues.
—Elizabeth Taylor

Aim above morality. Be not simply good; be good for something.
—Henry David Thoreau

Spiritually, I feel that people have a need to give
back. To whom much is given, much is required.
—Cynthia Presley

The time is always right to do what is right.
—Martin Luther King, Jr.

Judge not, that ye not be judged.
—Matthew 7:1

OPEN-MINDEDNESS

I call that mind free, which sets no bounds to its love,
which is not imprisoned in itself or in a sect, which
recognizes in all human beings the image of God.
—William Ellery Channing

A closed mind is a dying mind.
—Edna Ferber

Where there is an open mind, there will always be a frontier.
—Charles F. Kettering

I learned to make my mind large, as the universe
is large, so there is room for paradoxes.
—Maxine Hong Kingston

I would rather have a mind opened by
wonder than one closed by belief.
—Gerry Spence

OPPRESSION

Find out just what any people will quietly submit to and
you have found out the exact measure of injustice
and wrong which will be imposed upon them.
—Frederick Douglass

You can't hold a man down without staying down with him.
—Booker T. Washington

Racism and oppression have traditionally been
synonymous with good business practice for America.
—Beverly J. Hawkins

If tyranny and oppression come to this land, it
will be in the guise of fighting a foreign enemy.
—James Madison

If you want a picture of the future, imagine
a boot stamping on a human face—forever.
—George Orwell

People in distress will sometimes prefer a
problem that is familiar to a solution that is not.
—Neil Postman

As nightfall does not come all at once, neither does oppression.
—William O. Douglas

Where today are the Pequot? Where are the Narragansett, the
Mohican, the Pcanet, and other powerful tribes of our people?
They have vanished before the avarice and oppression of
the white man, as snow before the summer sun.
—Tecumseh

Class supremacy, male supremacy, white
supremacy—it's all the same game.
—Coletta Reid

None are more hopelessly enslaved than
those who falsely believe they are free.
—Johann von Goethe

Oppression does not remain static. It
carries the seed of its own destruction.
—Ann Sewell

ORGANIZATION & MANAGEMENT

Hierarchies make some people dependent on others, blame the dependent for their dependency, and then use that dependency as a justification for further exercise of authority.
—Martha Ackelsberg

Meetings are an addictive, highly self-indulgent activity that corporations and other large organizations habitually engage in only because they cannot actually masturbate.
—Dave Barry

Today the large corporation is lord and master, and most of its employees have been desensitized much as were the medieval peasants who never knew they were serfs.
—Ralph Nader

We have created trouble for ourselves in organizations by confusing control with order.
—Margaret J. Wheatley

Organization, far from creating authority, is the only cure for it and the only means whereby each of us will get used to taking an active and conscious part in collective work, and cease being passive instruments in the hands of leaders.

—Errico Malatesta

A committee is a cul-de-sac down which ideas are lured and then quietly strangled.

—Barnett Cocks

Bad administration, to be sure, can destroy good policy; but good administration can never save bad policy.

—Adlai Stevenson

I have come to realize that every management act is a political act. By this I mean that every management act in some way redistributes or reinforces power.

—Richard Farson

The trouble with organizing a thing is that pretty soon folks get to paying more attention to the organization than what they're organized for.

—Laura Ingalls Wilder

An efficient bureaucracy is the greatest threat to liberty.
—Eugene McCarthy

Why should workers agree to be slaves in a basically authoritarian structure? They should have control over it themselves. Why shouldn't communities have a dominant voice in running the institutions that affect their lives?
—Noam Chomsky

PARENTING

There are only two lasting bequests we can hope to give our children. One is roots; the other, wings.
—Hodding Carter

We often experience parental anger as a horrifying encounter with our worst selves.
—Nancy Samalin

Parents forgive their children least readily for the faults they themselves instilled in them.
—Marie von Ebner-Eschenbach

How sad that men would base an entire civilization on the principle of paternity, upon legal ownership and presumed responsibility for children, and then never really get to know their sons and daughters very well.
—Phyllis Chesler

Nothing has a stronger influence…on children, than the unlived life of the parent.
—Carl G. Jung

Most of us have become parents long before we have stopped being children.
—Mignon McLaughlin

If you bungle raising your children, I don't think whatever else you do matters very much.
—Jacqueline Kennedy Onassis

Biology is the least of what makes someone a mother.
—Oprah Winfrey

PATRIOT ACT

For the first time in our history, American citizens have been
seized by the executive branch of government and put in
prison without being charged with a crime, without having
the right to a trial, without being able to see a lawyer,
and without even being able to contact their families.

—Al Gore

Ordinary Americans should not have to worry that the FBI is rifling
through their medical records, seizing their personal papers, or
forcing charities and advocacy groups to divulge membership lists.

—Ann Beeson

You're not going to win the war on terrorism if you destroy who
we are as Americans and take away our rights and liberties.

—Wesley Clark

We believe these civil liberties [freedom of speech, assembly,
and privacy; equality before the law; due process; and freedom
from unreasonable searches and seizures] are now
threatened by the USA Patriot Act.

—City of Cambridge Resolution

One nation under surveillance.
—Protest sign

Calling this the Patriot Act is quite a dangerous action within itself, because the implication follows: If you speak against the Patriot Act, well, you sure aren't being a good citizen in our country's time of need. When Bush labels his actions as the model of patriotism, he then classifies all dissent as un-American.
—Michael Moore

WARNING: Although the Santa Cruz Library makes every effort to protect your privacy, under the federal USA Patriot Act (Public Law 107-56), records of the books and other materials you borrow from this library may be obtained by federal agents. That federal law prohibits library workers from informing you if federal agents have obtained records about you.
—Sign posted at Santa Cruz Library

PATRIOTISM

The love of one's country is a splendid thing.
But why should love stop at the border?
—Pablo Casals

"My country, right or wrong," is a thing no patriot
would think of saying except in a desperate case.
It is like saying, "My mother, drunk or sober."
—G. K. Chesterton

The nationalist not only does not disapprove of atrocities
committed by his own side, but he has a remarkable
capacity for not even hearing about them.
—George Orwell

Conceit, arrogance, and egotism are the essentials of
patriotism…. Patriotism assumes that our globe is divided
into little spots, each one surrounded by an iron gate. Those
who had the fortune of being born on some particular spot,
consider themselves better, nobler, grander, more intelligent
than the living beings inhabiting any other spot.
—Emma Goldman

To believe that patriotism will not flourish if patriotic
ceremonies are voluntary and spontaneous, instead of a
compulsory routine, is to make an unflattering estimate
of the appeal of our institutions to free minds.
—Robert H. Jackson

Blind faith in bad leadership is not patriotism.
—Protest sign

The highest patriotism is not a blind acceptance of
official policy, but a love of one's country deep
enough to call her to a higher standard.
—George McGovern

One nation under surveillance.
—Protest sign

I love my country.... I particularly cherish its civic ideals—
social equality, individual liberty, a populist democracy—
and the unending struggle to put their laudable, if
often contradictory, claims into practice.
—Michael Kazin

To announce that there must be no criticism of the
president, or that we are to stand by the president,
right or wrong, is not only unpatriotic and servile,
but is morally treasonable to the American public.
—Theodore Roosevelt

PEACE

Peace can only last where human rights are respected, where people are fed, and where individuals and nations are free.
—Dalai Lama

Blessed are the peacemakers, for they shall be called sons of God.
—Matthew 5:9

Nation shall not lift up sword against nation,
neither shall they learn war any more.
—Isaiah 2:4

There are causes worth dying for, but none worth killing for.
—Albert Camus

Peace is not a passive but an active condition, not a negation but an affirmation. It is a gesture as strong as war.
—Mary Roberts Rinehart

Nonviolence is a powerful and just weapon, which cuts without wounding and ennobles those who wield it. It's a sword that heals.
—Martin Luther King, Jr.

There is no way to peace. Peace is the way.
—A. J. Muste

The only way to abolish war is to make peace heroic.
—John Dewey

Peace cannot be kept by force. It can
only be achieved by understanding.
—Albert Einstein

What difference does it make to the dead, the orphans, and the
homeless, whether the mad destruction is wrought under the
name of totalitarianism or the holy name of liberty or democracy?
—Mahatma Gandhi

All men desire peace, but few desire
the things that make for peace.
—Thomas à Kempis

Peace is not an absence of war; it is a virtue, a state of
mind, a disposition for benevolence, confidence, justice.
—Baruch Spinoza

Nothing can bring you peace but yourself.
—Ralph Waldo Emerson

POLITICS

In politics, an organized minority is a political majority.
—Jesse Jackson

You can't ignore politics, no matter how much you'd like to.
—Molly Ivins

Politics is the art of looking for trouble, finding it whether it exists or not, diagnosing it incorrectly, and applying the wrong remedy.
—Ernest Benn

You campaign in poetry. You govern in prose.
—Mario Cuomo

Political extremism involves two prime ingredients: an excessively simple diagnosis of the world's ills, and a conviction that there are identifiable villains back of it all.
—John W. Gardner

When I entered politics, I took the only downward
turn you could take from journalism.
—Jim Hightower

Politics. From the Greek "poly," meaning many,
and "ticks," a small, annoying bloodsucker.
—Dave Barry

All politics is local.
—Tip O'Neill

Politics is an act of faith; you have to show some kind of
confidence in the intellectual and moral capacity of the public.
—George McGovern

To the youth of America, I say, beware of being trivialized
by the commercial culture that tempts you daily.... If
you do not turn onto politics, politics will turn on you.
—Ralph Nader

Politics hates a vacuum. If it isn't filled
with hope, someone will fill it with fear.
—Naomi Klein

Political language—and with variations this is true of all political
parties, from Conservatives to Anarchists—is designed to
make lies sound truthful and murder respectable, and to
give the appearance of solidity to pure wind.
—George Orwell

The political is the personal.
—Gloria Steinem

Today's public figures can no longer write their
own speeches or books, and there is some
evidence that they can't read them, either.
—Gore Vidal

POVERTY

I used to think I was poor. Then they told me I was not
poor, I was needy. They told me it was self-defeating to
think of myself as needy, I was deprived. Then they told me
underprivileged was overused. I was disadvantaged. I still
do not have a dime, but I have a great vocabulary.
—Jules Feiffer

What would you think of me if I were capable of seating myself at a table and gorging myself with food and saw about me the children of my fellow beings starving to death?
—Eugene V. Debs

The reason we are fighting the war on drugs is because we lost the war on poverty.
—Sargent Shriver

The war against hunger is truly mankind's war of liberation.
—John F. Kennedy

I don't believe that it's true that the poor will always be with us. I think that kind of pious fatalism is just an excuse for keeping things the way they are.
—Margaret Culkin Banning

The poverty of our century is unlike that of any other. It is not, as poverty was before, the result of natural scarcity, but of a set of priorities imposed upon the rest of the world by the rich. Consequently, the modern poor are not pitied…but written off as trash.
—John Berger

This administration today, here and now, declares
unconditional war on poverty in America.
—Lyndon B. Johnson

Many of us regard ourselves as mildly liberal or centrist politically,
voice fairly pleasant sentiments about our poor children, contribute
money to send poor kids to summer camp, feel benevolent....
Meanwhile, we put other people's children into an economic and
environmental death zone and say to ourselves, "Well, I hope that
they don't kill each other off. But if they do, it's not my fault."
—Jonathan Kozol

People who claw their way to the top are not likely to find very
much wrong with the system that enabled them to rise.
—Arthur Schlesinger, Jr.

We know that a peaceful world cannot long
exist one-third rich and two-thirds hungry.
—Jimmy Carter

Poverty is the worst form of violence.
—Mahatma Gandhi

America is an enormous frosted cupcake in
the middle of millions of starving people.
—Gloria Steinem

There is no such thing as an acceptable level of unemployment,
because hunger is not acceptable, poverty is not acceptable, poor
health is not acceptable, and a ruined life is not acceptable.
—Hubert H. Humphrey

POWER

The obligation of accepting a position of power
is to be, above all else, a good human being.
—Peter Block

He who is morally impressed by power is never in a
critical mood, and he is never a revolutionary character.
—Erich Fromm

Beware of dissipating your powers; strive
constantly to concentrate them.
—Johann von Goethe

The most common way people give up their
power is by thinking they don't have any.
—Alice Walker

Nowhere does power give itself up willingly.
—Nan Levinson

All things are subject to interpretation whichever interpretation
prevails at a given time is a function of power and not truth.
—Friedrich Nietzsche

Openly questioning the way the world works and challenging the
power of the powerful is not an activity customarily rewarded.
—Dale Splendor

Of all the manifestations of power,
restraint impresses men the most.
—Thucydides

The lust for power is not rooted in strength, but in weakness.
—Erich Fromm

PRIVACY

Privacy is granted to you by others, by their decency,
by their understanding, by their compassionate
behavior, by the laws of the land.
—Alida Brill

The right to be let alone is indeed the beginning of all freedom.
—William O. Douglas

The Constitution is not an instrument for the government to
restrain the people, it is an instrument for the people to restrain
the government—lest it come to dominate our lives and interests.
—Patrick Henry

The history of this country was made largely
by people who wanted to be left alone.
—Eric Hoffer

Today, the degradation of the inner life is symbolized by the fact
that the only place sacred from interruption is the private toilet.
—Lewis Mumford

The human animal needs a freedom seldom mentioned, freedom from intrusion. He needs a little privacy quite as much as he wants understanding or vitamins or exercise or praise.
—Phyllis McGinley

Big Brother is watching you.
—George Orwell

Civilization is the progress toward a society of privacy. The savage's whole existence is public, ruled the laws of his tribe. Civilization is the process of setting man free from men.
—Ayn Rand

PROGRESS

Progress is not automatic; the world grows better because people wish that it should, and take the right steps to make it better.
—Jane Addams

I do not believe in the indefinite progress for society as a whole. I believe in man's improvement in himself.
—Balzac

If there is no struggle, there is no progress.
—Frederick Douglass

The only principle that does not inhibit progress is: anything goes.
—Paul Feyerabend

Progress is a nice word. But change is its
motivator. And change has its enemies.
—Robert F. Kennedy

Is it progress if a cannibal uses a fork?
—Stanislaw J. Lec

There are many ways of going forward,
but only one way of standing still.
—Franklin D. Roosevelt

All progress has resulted from people
who took unpopular positions.
—Adlai Stevenson

The art of progress is to preserve order amid
change, and to preserve change amid order.
—Alfred North Whitehead

The reasonable man adapts himself to the world; the unreasonable
one persists in trying to adapt the world to himself. Therefore
all progress depends on the unreasonable man.
—George Bernard Shaw

Human progress is neither automatic nor inevitable.
—Martin Luther King, Jr.

PROTEST

The dissident does not operate in the realm of genuine power at
all. He is not seeking power. He has no desire for office and does
not gather votes. He does not attempt to charm the public, he
offers nothing and promises nothing…. His actions simply
articulate his dignity as a citizen, regardless of the cost.
—Vaclav Havel

Nothing wrong with a few professional protesters,
when the world is full of professional oppressors.
—Alan Bamford

One who breaks an unjust law that conscience tells him is unjust,
and who willingly accepts the penalty of imprisonment in order to
arouse the conscience of the community over its injustice, is
in reality expressing the highest respect for law.
—Martin Luther King, Jr.

If you want a symbolic gesture, don't burn the flag; wash it.
—Norman Thomas

I am a student. Please do not fold, spindle, or mutilate me.
—Slogan of the 1964 Free Speech Movement

PUNISHMENT

No punishment has ever possessed enough power
of deterrence to prevent the commission of crimes.
—Hannah Arendt

Prisons don't rehabilitate, they don't punish, they
don't protect—so what the hell do they do?
—Jerry Brown

I hear much of people's calling out to punish the guilty,
but very few are concerned to clear the innocent.
—Daniel DeFoe

Men are not punished for their sins, but by them.
—Elbert Hubbard

Penalties serve to deter those who are
not inclined to commit any crimes.
—Karl Kraus

For the same criminal behavior, the poor are more likely to be
arrested; if arrested, they are more likely to be charged; if charged,
more likely to be convicted; if convicted, more likely to be
sentenced to prison; and if sentenced, more likely to be given
longer prison terms than members of the middle and upper classes.
—Jeffrey Reiman

The reformative effect of punishment is a belief that dies hard,
I think, because it is so satisfying to our sadistic impulses.
—Bertrand Russell

Distrust all in whom the impulse to punish is powerful.
—Friedrich Nietzsche

RACISM

I got nothing against no Viet Cong. No
Vietnamese ever called me a nigger.
—Muhammad Ali

When blacks are unemployed, they are considered
lazy and apathetic. When whites are unemployed,
it's considered a depression.
—Jesse Jackson

Racism is man's gravest threat to man—the
maximum of hatred for a minimum of reason.
—Abraham Joshua Heschel

In order to get beyond racism, we must first
take account of race. There is no other way.
—Harry Blackmun

All white people, I think, are implicated in [racism] so
long as we participate in America in a normal way
and attempt to go on leading normal lives while
any one race is being cheated and tormented.
—Jonathan Kozol

Violence is black children going to school for twelve
years and receiving six years' worth of education.
—Julian Bond

Racism is so universal in this country, so widespread and
deep-seated, that it is invisible because it is so normal.
—Shirley Chisholm

Whenever I hear anyone arguing for slavery, I feel a
strong impulse to see it tried on him personally.
—Abraham Lincoln

Let's call the drug war what it is—ethnic cleansing of Americans.
—Jello Biafra

We are not fighting for integration, nor are we fighting for separation. We are fighting for recognition as human beings.
—Malcolm X

We didn't land on Plymouth Rock, my brothers and sisters—Plymouth Rock landed on us.
—Malcolm X

The pursuit of otherness, the sense that we are somehow different than our brothers and sisters, no matter where we find them, allows for all the other great evils: racism, sexism, homophobia, violence against gay people and against women.
—Anna Quindlen

My father was a slave and my people died to build this country, and I'm going to stay right here and have a part of it, just like you. And no fascist-minded people like you will drive me from it. Is that clear?
—Paul Robeson

RADICAL RIGHT

Hasn't America seen enough of the exclusionary, prejudicial,
vote-suppressing, racial-profiling, inner city–ignoring,
confederate flag–waving, Bob Jones University–
loving attitudes of the radical right?

—Patrick Kennedy

There is no place in our world for an ideology that
seeks to close minds, force obedience, and return
the world to a paradise that never was.

—Tim Berra

The theocratic right's ideal is an authoritarian
society where Christian men interpret God's will as
law. Women are helpmates, and children are the property
of their parents. Earth must submit to the dominion of those
to whom God has granted power. People are basically sinful,
and must be restrained by harsh punitive laws. Social problems
are caused by satanic conspiracies aided and abetted by
liberals, homosexuals, feminists, and secular humanists.

—Chip Berlet & Margaret Quigley

We live in a historical period when the fanaticism of America is on the right, and it has the apparatus to support it.
—Bill Clinton

During my opposition to the Vietnam War, the religious segment of the Radical Right attacked not only my patriotism, but the authenticity of my personal Christian faith. It is a tactic of the Radical Right to impugn the personality and character of its foes.
—Mark O. Hatfield

We cannot let the right wing roll back more than thirty years of social progress.
—Barbra Streisand

I'm gonna agree with Mrs. Clinton. There *is* a vast right-wing conspiracy in this country, but it's not hidden. It's right out there in plain sight.
—Molly Ivins

I'm frankly sick and tired of the political preachers across this country telling me as a citizen that if I want to be a moral person, I must believe in A, B, C, and D.
—Barry Goldwater

REBELLION & STRUGGLE

You can imprison a man, but not an idea. You can exile a man, but not an idea. You can kill a man, but not an idea.

—Benazir Bhutto

In order to exist, man must rebel.

—Albert Camus

What is a rebel? A man who says no.

—Albert Camus

This struggle of people against their conditions, this where you find the meaning in life.

—Rose Chernin

Anarchism is a tendency in the history of human thought and action which seeks to identify coercive, authoritarian, and hierarchic structures of all kinds and to challenge their legitimacy—and if they cannot justify their legitimacy, which is quite commonly the case, to work to undermine them and expand the scope of freedom.

—Noam Chomsky

The way to find what the mainstream will do tomorrow
is to associate with the lunatic fringe today.
—Jean-Louis Gassee

The system of education and employment works to redefine who
you are in the deepest sense, pushing you away from developing
and acting upon your own vision and guiding ideas. Hence, if
you want to stand for something and avoid vanishing as an
independent force in society, you have no choice but to resist.
—Jeff Schmidt

Chaos is not brought about by rebellion; it is
brought about by the absence of political struggle.
—Susan Sherman

Disobedience, in the eyes of anyone who has read history, is
man's original virtue. It is through disobedience that progress
has been made, through disobedience and rebellion.
—Oscar Wilde

Never doubt that a small group of thoughtful, committed citizens
could change the world. Indeed, it's the only thing that ever has.
—Margaret Mead

It is dangerous to be right when the government is wrong.
—François Voltaire

RELIGION

Scriptures, n. The sacred books of our holy religion, as
distinguished from the false and profane writings
on which all other faiths are based.
—Ambrose Bierce

Religion is sort of like a lift in your shoes. If it makes you
feel better, fine. Just don't ask me to wear your shoes.
—George Carlin

We are not the animal with tools or the animal with advanced
language; we are the religious animal. Because we know that
we are going to die, we question what life means.
—Forrester Church

When we blindly adopt a religion, a political
system, a literary dogma, we become automatons.
—Anaïs Nin

Wandering in a vast forest at night, I have only a faint light
to guide me. A stranger appears and says to me: "My friend,
you should blow out your candle in order to find your
way more clearly." This stranger is a theologian.

—Denis Diderot

Real religion should be something that liberates men.
But churches don't want free men who can think for
themselves and find their own divinity within.

—Federico Fellini

I do benefits for all religions—I'd hate
to blow the hereafter on a technicality.

—Bob Hope

I am a Hindu. I am also a Muslim. I am also a Jew and a Christian.
Some would even say I'm an atheist. Religion and the color of
one's skin—what useless ways to define and establish a nation!

—Mahatma Gandhi

A person has no religion who has not slowly
and painfully gathered one together.

—D. H. Lawrence

Blind obedience is a sure sign of trouble. The likelihood of religion becoming evil is greatly diminished when there is freedom for individual thinking and when honest inquiry is encouraged.
—Charles Kimball

Since I have heard often enough that everyone in the end has his own religion, nothing seemed more natural to me than to fashion my own.
—Johann von Goethe

Being religious means asking passionately the question of the meaning of our existence and being willing to receive answers, even if the answers hurt.
—Paul Tillich

Religion is a candle inside a multicolored lantern. Everyone looks through a particular color, but the candle is always there.
—Mohammed Neguib

Advocates of religiosity extol the virtues or moral habits that religion is supposed to instill in us. But we should be equally concerned with the intellectual habits it discourages.
—Wendy Kaminer

True religion is a revolutionary force: it is an inveterate
enemy of oppression, privilege, and injustice.

—Sarvepalli Radhakrishnan

Once there was a time when all people believed in God
and the church ruled. This time is called the Dark Ages.

—George Bernard Shaw

Religion consists in a set of things which the average
man thinks he believes and wishes he were certain.

—Mark Twain

REPRODUCTIVE RIGHTS

In the last half of the twentieth century, the greatest advancement
in women's health was not made in an operating room or research
laboratory, but instead in the Supreme Court in 1972.

—Anat Maytal

[*Roe v. Wade*] was a necessary step
toward the full emancipation of women.

—Harry A. Blackmun

If men could get pregnant, abortion would be a sacrament.
—Florynce Kennedy

If the right to privacy means anything, it is the right of the
individual, married or single, to be free from unwanted
governmental intrusion into matters so fundamentally
affecting a person as the decision to bear or beget a child.
—William Brennan

Abortion should be safe, legal, and rare.
—Bill Clinton

Being pro-choice is not being pro-abortion. Being pro-choice
is trusting the individual to make the right decision for
herself and her family, and not entrusting that decision
to anyone wearing the authority of government.
—Hillary Rodham Clinton

[A woman's right to choose an abortion is] something central
to a woman's life, to her dignity…. And when government
controls that decision for her, she's being treated as less than
a full adult human being responsible for her own choices.
—Ruth Bader Ginsburg

Abortion is a deeply personal decision which ought to be
made between the patient, the family, and physician.
It's none of the government's business.

—Howard Dean

I will choose what enters me, what becomes flesh of my
flesh. Without choice, no politics, no ethics lives. I am not your
cornfield, not your uranium mine, not your calf for fattening, not
your cow for milking. You may not use me as your factory.

—Marge Piercy

No woman can call herself free who
does not own and control her body.

—Margaret Sanger

Against abortion? Don't have one.

—Unknown

REPUBLICANS

Republicans want smaller government for the same reason
crooks want fewer cops: it's easier to get away with murder.

—James Carville

If you want to live like a Republican,
you've got to vote for the Democrats.
—Dick Gephardt

Republican comes in the dictionary just
after reptile and just above repugnant.
—Julia Roberts

I've never understood that about Republicans. Even when they win,
they manage to come off sounding like an oppressed minority.
—Eric Holeman

Republicans (I think to myself) are conservatives who think it would
be best if we faced the fact that people are no damned good.
—Andy Rooney

The Republicans love to say that the Democratic Party is
ruled by "special interests." But when pressed to name these
"special interests," the usual reply is women, blacks, teachers,
and unions. Together they comprise the majority of Americans.
What about the "special interests" that dominate the
Republican Party, the oil companies, the banks, the gun
lobby, and the apostles of religious intolerance?
—Geraldine Ferraro

Republicans used to be the party that opposed social engineering, but now they push programs to outlaw marriage for some people, and encourage it for others.
—Bill Maher

When voters are given a choice between voting for a Republican or a Democrat who acts like a Republican, they'll vote for the Republican every time.
—Harry S. Truman

Give the Republicans credit. They know what they stand for. Tax cuts. Guns. Bombs. Oil. Big business. Old-boy networks. Privatization. Plundering the earth. Pillorying and padlocking the poor. Party-line votes.
—Derrick Z. Jackson

RESPONSIBILITY

The salvation of this human world lies nowhere else than in the human heart, in the human power to reflect, in human meekness and human responsibility.
—Vaclav Havel

I don't think of myself as a poor deprived ghetto girl who made good. I think of myself as somebody who from an early age knew I was responsible for myself, and I had to make good.
—Oprah Winfrey

Take your life in your hands, and what happens? A terrible thing: no one to blame.
—Erica Jong

We create our fate every day…most of the ills we suffer from are directly traceable to our own behavior.
—Henry Miller

People spend too much time finding other people to blame, too much energy finding excuses for not being what they are capable of being, and not enough energy getting on with their lives.
—J. Michael Straczynski

SCIENCE & CREATIONISM

Man is descended from a hairy, tailed quadruped, probably arboreal in its habits.
—Charles Darwin

Science has proof without any certainty.
Creationists have certainty without any proof.
—Ashley Montague

I would defend the liberty of consenting adult creationists
to practice whatever intellectual perversions they like in
the privacy of their own homes; but it is also necessary
to protect the young and innocent.
—Arthur C. Clarke

Science cannot resolve moral conflicts, but it can help to
more accurately frame the debates about those conflicts.
—Heinz Pagels

The American creationist movement has entirely bypassed the
scientific forum and has concentrated instead on political lobbying
and on taking its case to a fair-minded electorate…. The reason
for this strategy is overwhelmingly apparent: no scientific
case can be made for the theories they advance.
—Kenneth R. Miller

SECULARISM

Religion is good for American politics…when it accepts the principles of tolerance and pluralism; when it appeals to a shared sense of morality…. Religion is bad for American politics when it undermines the civil religion; when it speaks of political matters with the certitude of faith, in a pluralistic society in which faith cannot be used as a political standard; when it treats opponents as agents of Satan.
—Jim Castelli

Our government is not founded upon the rights of gods, but upon the rights of men. Our Constitution was framed, not to declare and uphold the deity of Christ, but the sacredness of humanity. Ours is the first government made by the people for the people.
—Robert Ingersoll

Nothing is more fallacious or inimical to genuine religious liberty than the seductive notion that the state should "favor" or "foster" religion. All history testifies that such practices inevitably result in favoring one religion over less powerful minorities and secular opinion.
—Edward L. Ericson

Human rights is not a religious idea. It is a secular idea, the product of the last four centuries of Western history.
—Arthur Schlesinger, Jr.

I can think of no greater disaster to this country than to have the voters of it divide upon religious lines.
—Alfred E. Smith

The present trend to repudiate the concept of America as a secular state and officially identify this nation with God and certain sectarian religious views does not bode well for religious pluralism in the United States, in which virtually all of the world's religions are represented among its citizens.
—James E. Wood

SECURITY

The only real security is not insurance or money or a job, not a house and furniture paid for, or a retirement fund, and never is it another person. It is the skill and humor and courage within, the ability to build your own fires and find your own peace.
—Audrey Sutherland

I tell you that man is tormented by no greater anxiety than to find
someone to whom he can hand over quickly [the] gift of freedom.
—Fyodor Dostoevsky

Only in growth, reform, and change, paradoxically
enough, is true security to be found.
—Anne Morrow Lindbergh

Americans used to roar like lions for liberty;
now we bleat like sheep for security.
—Norman Vincent Peale

Beware of the words "internal security,"
for they are the eternal cry of the oppressor.
—François Voltaire

There is no inverse relationship between freedom and
security. Less of one does not lead to more of the other.
People with no rights are not safe from terrorist attack.
—Molly Ivins

Security is not the meaning of my life.
Great opportunities are worth the risk.
—Shirley Hufstedler

SELF

In the depth of winter, I finally learned that
within me there lay an invincible summer.
—Albert Camus

What lies behind us and what lies before us are
tiny matters compared to what lies within us.
—Ralph Waldo Emerson

Be a first-rate version of yourself, not a
second-rate version of someone else.
—Judy Garland

There is nothing like returning to a place that remains unchanged
to find the ways in which you yourself have altered.
—Nelson Mandela

What we truly and earnestly aspire to be, that in some
sense we are. The mere aspiration, by changing the
frame of the mind, for the moment realizes itself.
—Anna Jameson

Until we can understand the assumptions in
which we are drenched, we cannot know ourselves.
—Adrienne Rich

Don't compromise yourself. You are all you've got.
—Janis Joplin

Everything that irritates us about others can
lead us to an understanding of ourselves.
—Carl G. Jung

When I let go of what I am, I become what I might be.
—Lao Tzu

Every extreme attitude is a flight from the self.
—Eric Hoffer

SERVICE

What do we live for, if not to make
life less difficult for each other?
—George Eliot

Ask not what your country can do for you,
but what you can do for your country.
—John F. Kennedy

Everyone can be great because anyone can serve. You don't
have to have a college degree to serve. You don't even have
to make your subject and your verb agree to serve....You
only need a heart full of grace. A soul generated by love.
—Martin Luther King, Jr.

I don't know what your destiny will be, but one thing I do
know: the only ones among you who will be really happy
are those who have sought and found how to serve.
—Albert Schweitzer

Nothing liberates our greatness like
the desire to help, the desire to serve.
—Marianne Williamson

The best way to find yourself is to lose
yourself in the service of others.
—Mahatma Gandhi

SEX

Sex without love is an empty experience, but,
as empty experiences go, it's one of the best.
—Woody Allen

I've looked on a lot of women with lust. I've committed adultery in
my heart many times. God knows I will do this and forgives me.
—Jimmy Carter

Women complain about sex more than men. Their gripes
fall into two major categories: (1) Not enough. (2) Too much.
—Ann Landers

Sex is hardly ever just about sex.
—Shirley MacLaine

It's only premarital sex if you're going to get married.
—Unknown

I think on-stage nudity is disgusting, shameful, and
damaging to all things American. But if I were twenty-
two with a great body, it would be artistic, tasteful,

patriotic, and a progressive religious experience.
—**Shelley Winters**

God gave us a penis and a brain, but
only enough blood to run one at a time.
—**Robin Williams**

When authorities warn you of the sinfulness of
sex, there is an important lesson to be learned.
Do not have sex with the authorities.
—**Matt Groening**

SEXISM

When a man gives his opinion, he's a man.
When a woman gives her opinion, she's a bitch.
—**Bette Davis**

Sexism is the foundation on which all tyranny
is built. Every social form of hierarchy and abuse
is modeled on male-over-female domination.
—**Andrea Dworkin**

If you have any doubts that we live in a society controlled by men, try reading down the index of contributors to a volume of quotations, looking for women's names.
—Elaine Gill

Nobody objects to a woman being a good writer or sculptor or geneticist as long as she manages also to be a good wife, mother, good-looking, good-tempered, well-dressed, well-groomed, unaggressive.
—Marya Mannes

SILENCE

Learn to be quiet enough to hear the sound of the genuine within yourself, so that you can hear it in other people.
—Marian Wright Edelman

When you take my time you take something I had meant to use.
—Marianne Moore

You have not converted a man because you have silenced him.
—John Morley

In the end, we will remember not the words of
our enemies, but the silence of our friends.
—Martin Luther King, Jr.

Many a time I have wanted to stop talking
and find out what I really believed.
—Walter Lippmann

People who know little are usually great
talkers, while men who know much say little.
—Jean-Jacques Rousseau

In quiet places, reason abounds.
—Adlai Stevenson

Those who know don't talk. Those who talk don't know.
—Lao Tzu

SIMPLICITY

In character, in manners, in style, in all
things, the supreme excellence is simplicity.
—Henry Wadsworth Longfellow

The greatest truths are the simplest.
—A. W. Hare

Any intelligent fool can make things bigger, more complex,
and more violent. It takes a touch of genius—and a
lot of courage—to move in the opposite direction.
—Albert Einstein

A little simplification would be the first step toward rational living.
—Eleanor Roosevelt

Don't try so hard to be interesting, keep your distance, be honest,
fight the desire to be thought fascinating by the outside world.
—Etty Hillesum

Our life is frittered away by detail…simplify, simplify.
—Henry David Thoreau

I went to the woods because I wished to live deliberately,
to front only the essential facts of life, and see if I
could not learn what it had to teach, and not, when
I came to die, discover that I had not lived.
—Henry David Thoreau

Things which matter most should never be at
the mercy of things which matter least.
—Johann von Goethe

The wisdom of life consists in the elimination of nonessentials.
—Lin Yutang

The aspects of a thing that are most important to us are
hidden to us because of their simplicity and familiarity.
—Ludwig Wittgenstein

We have grown literally afraid to be poor. We despise anyone who
elects to be poor in order to simplify and save his inner life. If he
does not join the general scramble and pant with the money-
making street, we deem him spiritless and lacking in ambition.
—William James

THE SIXTIES

People today are still living off the table scraps of the sixties.
They are still being passed around—the music and the ideas.
—Bob Dylan

Hell no, we won't go.
—Anti-war slogan regarding Vietnam

The freedom that women were supposed to have found
in the sixties largely boiled down to easy contraception
and abortion; things to make life easier for men, in fact.
—Julie Burchill

The 1960s were when hallucinogenic drugs were really
big. And I don't think it's a coincidence that we
had the shows then like *The Flying Nun.*
—Ellen DeGeneres

I do my thing, and you do your thing. I am not in this world
to live up to your expectations, and you are not in this
world to live up to mine. You are you, and I am I, and
if by chance we find each other, it's beautiful.
—Frederick E. Perl

Obscene is not the picture of a naked woman who exposes
her pubic hair but that of a fully clad general who exposes
his medals rewarded in a war of aggression.
—Herbert Marcuse

If you can remember anything about
the sixties, you weren't really there.
—Paul Kantner

Make Love, Not War.
—Unknown

We have no honorable intentions in Vietnam.... Our
minimal expectation is to occupy it as an American colony.
—Martin Luther King, Jr.

If the sixties were truly "about" anything, it was the notion of a
decisive shift of power away from its traditional centers and
towards people who had been historically excluded....
From the rich to the poor, from the old to the young,
from the Right to the Left, from whites to blacks.
—Charles Shaar Murray

SOUL

To touch the soul of another human
being is to walk on holy ground.
—Stephen Covey

To dispose a soul to action we must upset its equilibrium.
—Eric Hoffer

The whole course of human history may depend on a change
of heart in a single, solitary, even humble individual. For it is
within the soul of the individual that the battle between
good and evil is waged and ultimately won or lost.
—Henry David Thoreau

You don't have a soul. You are a soul. You have a body.
—C. S. Lewis

The most important of life's battles is the one we
fight daily in the silent chambers of the soul.
—David O. McKay

The ability of the radical right to seize and exploit the terrain of
the soul has been helped immeasurably by the failure of the
rest of us [liberals] to even acknowledge the soul's existence.
—Anna Quindlen

O Lord, if there is a Lord, save my soul, if I have a soul.
—Ernest Renan

These are times that try men's souls.
—Thomas Paine

SPIRITUALITY

There is nothing so secular that it cannot be sacred.
—Madeleine L'Engle

The life of sensation is the life of greed; it requires
more and more. The life of the spirit requires less
and less; time is ample and its passage sweet.
—Annie Dillard

There are many, many gates to the sacred
and they are as wide as we need them to be.
—Sherry Anderson

The message of the United States is a spiritual message.
It is the message of human ideals; it is the message of
human dignity; it is the message of the freedom of ideas,
speech, press, the right to assemble, to worship, and
the message of freedom of movement of people.
—Hubert H. Humphrey

Spirituality is to religion as justice is to law.
—**Richard M. Gross**

Spirituality is rooted in desire. We long for something
we can neither name nor describe, but which is no less
real because of our inability to capture it with words.
—**Mary Jo Weaver**

Are all these events and circumstances of our lives truly
random and pointless, as agnostics and atheists would
argue? Or is there some deeper design in our lives, in
what happens to us in our work, in our relationships?
—**Robin Deen Carnes and Sally Craig**

SUCCESS

You've achieved success in your field when you don't
know whether what you're doing is work or play.
—**Warren Beatty**

It isn't success after all, is it, if it isn't
an expression of your deepest energies?
—**Marilyn French**

To laugh often and much, to win the respect of intelligent people
and the affection of children, to earn the appreciation of honest
critics and endure the betrayal of false friends, to appreciate
beauty, to find the best in others, to leave the world a bit better,
whether by a healthy child, a garden patch, or a redeemed
social condition, to know even one life has breathed easier
because you have lived. This is to have succeeded.
—Ralph Waldo Emerson

All successful men and women are big dreamers. They imagine
what their future could be, ideal in every respect, and then they
work every day toward their distant vision, that goal or purpose.
—Brian Tracy

Success is to be measured not so much by the position
that one has reached in life, as by the obstacles which
he has overcome while trying to succeed.
—Booker T. Washington

Why should we be in such desperate haste to succeed and in such
desperate enterprises? If a man does not keep pace with his
companions, perhaps it is because he hears a different drummer.
—Henry David Thoreau

To be successful, a woman has to be
much better at her job than a man.
—Golda Meir

TEACHING

You teach best what you most need to learn.
—Richard Bach

Teaching is not a lost art, but the regard for it is a lost tradition.
—Jacques Barzun

The best teacher is the one who suggests rather than dogmatizes,
and inspires his listener with the wish to teach himself.
—Edward Bulweer-Lytton

Teachers open the door, but you enter by yourself.
—Chinese proverb

When I transfer my knowledge, I teach.
When I transfer my beliefs, I indoctrinate.
—Arthur Danto

A teacher who is attempting to teach without inspiring the pupil
with a desire to learn is hammering on cold iron.

—Horace Mann

Teaching is mostly listening, and learning is mostly telling.

—Deborah Meier

What a teacher thinks she teaches often has
little to do with what students learn.

—Susan Ohanian

I cannot teach anybody anything. I can only make them think.

—Socrates

Education is an admirable thing, but it's well to remember from
time to time that nothing that is worth knowing can be taught.

—Oscar Wilde

Teacher-bashing has become a popular sport.... We blame teachers
for being unable to cure social ills that no one knows how to treat;
we insist that they instantly adopt whatever "solution" has most
recently been concocted by our national panacea machine.

—Parker Palmer

Experience teaches only the teachable.
—Aldous Huxley

TECHNOLOGY

Technology evolves so much faster than wisdom.
—Jennifer Stone

Sometimes decision-makers expect miracles and transformations to
follow the purchase and installation of equipment. This fondness
for tools and toys can be wasteful, foolish, and nonproductive.
—Jamie McKenzie

We share an American cultural bias that every problem we
face has a technical "fix," if only we can find it. That bias is
fostered by armies of experts who make a living "fixing" things.
—Parker Palmer

Perfection of means and confusion of goals seem—
in my opinion—to characterize our age.
—Albert Einstein

The Internet—Last Refuge of the Liberal.
—Ernest Partridge

All our inventions are but improved means to an unimproved end.
—Henry David Thoreau

Men have become the tools of their tools.
—Henry David Thoreau

We've all heard that a million monkeys banging
on a million typewriters will eventually reproduce
the entire works of Shakespeare. Now, thanks
to the Internet, we know this is not true.
—Robert Wilensky

TERRORISM

In my Cold War childhood, "godless communism" was the
unifying all-purpose enemy that justified everything from an
overkill arsenal of nuclear weapons to a host of unsavory allies.
Sept. 11…ushered in a new all-purpose enemy: terrorism.
—Ellen Goodman

Perhaps the biggest success in the War on Terror has been its
ability to distract the nation from the Corporate War on Us.
—Michael Moore

We all have to change. The world's poor cannot be led by people
like Mr. Bin Laden who think they can find their redemption in
our destruction. But the world's rich cannot be led by people
who play to our shortsighted selfishness, and pretend that we
can forever claim for ourselves what we do not for others.
—Bill Clinton

The war on terror cannot become a war on civil rights and
freedoms. We should not have to choose between securing our
homeland and securing the blessings of liberty. We can have both,
otherwise the terrorists have won, and we will not permit that.
—Howard Dean

The word "terrorist" has come to mean someone who is radical,
Islamic and foreign. But many believe we have as much to fear
from a home-grown group of anti-abortion crusaders.
—Jami Floyd

There are many reasons why human beings turn
to terrorism, but high among them is humiliation.
—H.D.S. Greenway

If you are a terror to many, then beware of many.
—Ausonius

"Terrorism" is what we call the violence of the
weak, and we condemn it; "war" is what we call
the violence of the strong, and we glorify it.
—Sydney J. Harris

Until Americans revisit their foreign policy practices and good
Muslims challenge distorted interpretations of Islam consistently,
we may not come out of the circle of terror and counterterror.
—Muqtedar Khan

It is crucial that civil liberties in this country be preserved,
otherwise, the terrorists will win the battle against
American values without firing another shot.
—Russ Feingold

THOUGHT

The significant problems we have cannot be solved at
the same level of thinking with which we created them.
—Albert Einstein

With our thoughts we make the world.
—Buddha

Men fear thought as they fear nothing else on earth, more
than ruin, more even than death…. Thought is subversive and
revolutionary, destructive and terrible, thought is merciless to
privilege, established institutions, and comfortable habit. Thought
looks into the pit of hell and is not afraid. Thought is great and
swift and free, the light of the world, and the chief glory of man.
—Bertrand Russell

I think, therefore I am.
—Rene Descartes

The most unpardonable sin in society is independence of thought.
—Emma Goldman

I think, therefore I'm single.
—Lizz Winstead

There's nothing I like less than bad
arguments for a view that I hold dear.
—Daniel Dennett

A great many people mistake opinions for thoughts.
—Herbert V. Prochnow

TOLERANCE

The test of courage comes when we are in the minority.
The test of tolerance comes when we are in the majority.
—Ralph W. Sockman

It rests with the liberals and the tolerant to preserve our
civilization. Everything of importance in this world has been
accomplished by the free inquiring spirit and the preservation
of that spirit is more important than any social system.
—John L. Lewis

Tolerance and understanding won't "trickle down"
in our society any more than wealth does.
—Muhammad Ali

Human diversity makes tolerance more than a
virtue; it makes it a requirement for survival.
—Rene Dubos

Intolerance is the most socially acceptable form of egotism, for it
permits us to assume superiority without personal boasting.
—Sidney J. Harris

Tolerance implies no lack of commitment to one's own beliefs.
Rather it condemns the oppression or persecution of others.
—John F. Kennedy

At one time, phrases such as Christian charity and
Christian tolerance were used to denote kindness
and compassion…. Now, Christian is invariably
linked to right-wing conservative political thought.
—Peter McWilliams

Even the word "tolerance" is intolerable.
No person has the right to tolerate another.
—Amalie Taubels

The capacity for getting along with our neighbor depends to a
large extent on the capacity for getting along with ourselves.
The self-respecting individual will try to be as tolerant of
his neighbor's shortcomings as he is of his own.
—Eric Hoffer

TRUTH

Pushing any truth out very far, you are met by a countertruth.
—Henry Ward Beecher

Men occasionally stumble over the truth, but most of them pick
themselves up and hurry off as if nothing ever happened.
—Winston Churchill

There are no whole truths: all truths are half-truths. It is
trying to treat them as whole truths that plays the devil.
—Alfred North Whitehead

Believe those who are seeking the truth; doubt those who find it.
—André Gide

In a time of universal deceit, telling the truth is a revolutionary act.
—George Orwell

When opinions are free, either in matters of government
or religion, truth will finally and powerfully prevail.
—Thomas Paine

All great truths begin as blasphemies.
—George Bernard Shaw

Truth always rests with the minority, while the strength of a
majority is illusory, formed by the gangs who have no opinion.
—Søren Kierkegaard

The truth is rarely pure and never simple.
—Oscar Wilde

We can build a community out of seekers of
truth, but not out of possessors of truth.
—William Sloane Coffin

VOTING

Vote. Get out and register other people to vote.
—Molly Ivins & Lou Dubose

The vote is the most powerful instrument ever devised by man for breaking down injustice and destroying the terrible walls which imprison men because they are different from other men.
—Lyndon Baines Johnson

Bad officials are elected by good citizens who do not vote.
—George Jean Nathan

Half of the American people have never read a newspaper. Half never voted for president. One hopes it is the same half.
—Gore Vidal

It's not the voting that's democracy, it's the counting.
—Tom Stoppard

WAR

Lying and war are always associated. Pay attention to
war-makers when they try to defend their current
war…if they move their lips, they're lying.
—Phil Berrigan

The grim fact is that we prepare for war like precocious
giants and for peace like retarded pygmies.
—Lester Pearson

Ours is a world of nuclear giants and ethical infants.
We know more about war than we know about peace,
more about killing than we know about living.
—Omar Bradley

I know not with what weapons World War III will be fought,
but World War IV will be fought with sticks and stones.
—Albert Einstein

The first casualty of war is truth.
—Rudyard Kipling

I hate war as only a soldier who has lived it can, only as one who has seen its brutality, its futility, its stupidity.
—Dwight D. Eisenhower

Every gun that is made, every warship launched, every rocket fired signifies, in the final sense, a theft from those who hunger and are not fed, those who are cold and are not clothed.
—Dwight D. Eisenhower

War does not determine who is right—only who is left.
—Bertrand Russell

War is Terrorism with a Bigger Budget.
—Peace rally sign

The means of war are inevitably horrible and the ends of war are always uncertain.
—Howard Zinn

When the rich make war it's the poor that die.
—Jean-Paul Sartre

The belief in the possibility of a short decisive war appears to be
one of the most ancient and dangerous of human illusions.
—Robert Lynd

War is only a cowardly escape from the problems of peace.
—Thomas Mann

A nation that continues year and year to spend more
money on military defense than on programs of
social uplift is approaching spiritual death.
—Martin Luther King, Jr.

I'm fed up to the ears with old men dreaming
up wars for young men to die in.
—George McGovern

The direct use of force is such a poor solution to any problem, it is
generally employed only by small children and large nations.
—David Friedman

War is the unfolding of miscalculations.
—Barbara Tuchman

WEALTH

That man is richest whose pleasures are cheapest.
—Henry David Thoreau

The superior person understands rightness;
the inferior person understands profit.
—Confucius

The rich are never threatened by the poor; they don't notice them.
—Marie de France

When a man tells you that he got rich
through hard work, ask him: "Whose?"
—Don Marquis

If you want to know what God thinks of
money, just look at the people he gave it to.
—Dorothy Parker

Wealth consists not in having great
possessions, but in having few wants.
—Epicurus

We can have democracy in this country or we can have great wealth concentrated in the hands of a few, but we can't have both.

—Louis Brandeis

When power or wealth concentrates too heavily in too few hands in society, democracy is useful for dispensing much of that power back to the people. Of course, those already in power bitterly resent this; that is why there is such a strong antidemocratic streak in wealthy conservatives and business owners. They complain that democracy allows the poor to legally steal from the rich.

—Steve Kangas

WISDOM

God, give us grace to accept with serenity the things that cannot be changed, courage to change the things which should be changed, and the wisdom to distinguish the one from the other.

—Reinhold Niebuhr

We don't receive wisdom; we must discover it ourselves after a journey that no one can take for us or spare us.

—Marcel Proust

Wisdom comes only through suffering.
—Aeschylus

Wisdom is not a product of schooling,
but of the lifelong attempt to acquire it.
—Albert Einstein

It is not the answer that enlightens, but the question.
—Eugene Ionesco

Little things affect little minds.
—Benjamin Disraeli

The wise man will not look for the faults of others,
nor for what they have done or left undone,
but will look rather to his own misdeeds.
—*The Dhammapada*

To be a philosopher is not merely to have subtle thoughts, nor even
to found a school, but so to love wisdom as to live according to its
dictates, a life of simplicity, independence, magnanimity, and trust.
—Henry David Thoreau

There is no wisdom equal to that which comes after the event.
—Geraldine Jewsbury

WOMEN & MEN

If a woman has to choose between catching a fly ball and
saving an infant's life, she will choose to save the infant's
life without even considering if there are men on base.
—Dave Barry

What is now called the nature of women is an eminently
artificial thing—the result of forced repression in some
directions, unnatural stimulation in others.
—John Stuart Mill

When women are depressed they either eat or go shopping. Men
invade another country. It's a whole different way of thinking.
—Elayne Boosler

One is not born a woman, but rather becomes one.
—Simone de Beauvoir

Male and female represent the two sides of the great radical dualism. But, in fact, they are perpetually passing into one another. Fluid hardens to solid, solid rushes to fluid. There is no wholly masculine man, no purely feminine woman.

—Margaret Fuller

Women speak because they wish to speak, whereas a man speaks only when driven to speech by something outside himself—like, for instance, he can't find any clean socks.

—Jean Kerr

WORK

I believe you are your work. Don't trade the stuff of your life—time—for nothing more than dollars. That's a rotten bargain.

—Rita Mae Brown

Diligence overcomes difficulties; sloth makes them.

—Benjamin Franklin

If you want to predict the future, create it.

—Peter Drucker

Your work is to discover your work and then
with all your heart give yourself to it.
—Buddha

The highest reward for a person's toil is not what
they get for it, but what they become by it.
—John Ruskin

We cannot wait for the storm to blow over;
we must learn to work in the rain.
—Jennifer Granholm

Everyone should carefully observe which way his heart
draws him, and then choose that way with all his strength.
—Hasidic saying

People just starting their careers may think a job is just a job. But
when they choose a company, they often choose a way of life.
—Terrence E. Deal and Allan A. Kennedy

I long to accomplish a great and noble task, but it is my chief duty
to accomplish small tasks as if they were great and noble.
—Helen Keller

If you want to build a ship, don't drum up the men to gather wood, divide the work, and give orders. Instead, teach them to yearn for the vast and endless sea.
—Antoine de Saint-Exupery

Never tell people how to do things. Tell them what to do and they will surprise you with their ingenuity.
—George S. Patton, Jr.

WRITERS AND WRITING

If you do not breathe through writing, if you do not cry out in writing, or sing in writing, then don't write, because our culture has no use for it.
—Anaïs Nin

Who is more to be pitied, a writer bound and gagged by policemen or one living in perfect freedom who has nothing more to say?
—Kurt Vonnegut

Writing is a certain way of wanting freedom.
—Jean-Paul Sartre

I write to discover what I think.
—Daniel Boorstin

I don't write fiction. I invent facts.
—Jorge Luis Borges

Better to write for yourself and have no public,
than to write for the public and have no self.
—Cyril Connolly

The most essential gift for a good writer is a built-in,
shock-proof shit detector. This is the writer's
radar and all great writers have had it.
—Ernest Hemingway

An author makes you notice, makes you pay attention, and this
is a great gift. My gratitude for good writing is unbounded;
I'm grateful for it the way I'm grateful for the ocean.
—Anne Lamott

As a writer you are free. You are in the country
where you make up the rules, the laws.
—Ursula K. Le Guin

Shocking and Stupid Quotations of the Right

ABSURDITY

It is particularly fitting to honor the Freedom President on this particular piece of coinage because, as has been pointed out, President Reagan was wounded under the left arm by a bullet that had ricocheted and flattened to the size of a dime.

—Mark Souder, Republican congressman, explaining why Reagan should replace Roosevelt on the dime.

The earth is flat, and anyone who disputes this claim is an atheist who deserves to be punished.

—Abdel-Aziz Ibn Baaz, sheik and Saudi Arabian religious authority, 1993

How can there be peace when drunkards, drug dealers, communists, atheists, New Age worshippers of Satan, secular humanists, oppressive dictators, greedy money changers, revolutionary assassins, adulterers, and homosexuals are on top?

—Pat Robertson, founder of the Christian Broadcasting Network and host of *The 700 Club*.

I'm telling you that President Bush is doing just what Jesus would have done.

—Bill O'Reilly

If life were to be found on a planet, then it would also have
been contaminated by original sin and would require salvation.
**—Piero Coda, Roman Catholic theologian, discussing
the possible need to evangelize extraterrestrials**

If I do not return to the pulpit this weekend,
millions of people will go to hell.
**—Jimmy Swaggart, televangelist caught with prostitute
and defrocked by the Assemblies of God church**

I'll submit to you that George W. Bush is the closest modern
president to what the Founding Fathers had in mind.
**—Bill O'Reilly, host of *The O'Reilly Factor*
on the conservative Fox News Channel**

ANTI-SEMITISM

Whether the Holocaust is real or not, the Jews clearly
have a motive for fostering the idea that it occurred.
Not only do they have a motive, but they have the
means with the media domination they now hold.
**—David Duke, former head of the Ku Klux Klan and elected
as a Republican to the Louisiana state legislature**

[The Antichrist] will be a full-grown counterfeit
of Christ. Of course he'll be Jewish.
—**Jerry Falwell, Baptist minister and founder of The Moral Majority**

Please get me the names of the Jews. You know,
the big Jewish contributors of the Democrats?
Could we please investigate these cocksuckers?
—**Richard M. Nixon, resigned the presidency
because of the Watergate scandal**

The god of Judaism is the devil. The Jew will not be recognized
by God as one of His chosen people until he abandons his
demonic religion and returns to the faith of his fathers—
the faith which embraces Jesus Christ and His Gospel.
—**David Chilton, author of *The Days of Vengeance***

ARROGANCE

I do not need to explain why I say things. That's the interesting
thing about being the president. Maybe somebody needs
to explain to me why they say something, but I don't
feel like I owe anybody an explanation.
—**George W. Bush**

I will never apologize for the United States
of America. I don't care what the facts are.
—George H. W. Bush, after a U.S. Navy warship shot down an
Iranian commercial airliner killing 290 civilians in 1988

I believe God wants me to be president,
but if that doesn't happen, it's OK.
—George W. Bush

Only the little people pay taxes.
—Leona Helmsley, businesswoman sentenced
to four years in prison for tax evasion

When the president does it, that means it is not illegal.
—Richard M. Nixon

BIGOTRY, CHAUVINISM, & THEOCRACY

I don't know that atheists should be considered citizens, nor
should they be considered patriots. This is one nation under God.
—George H. W. Bush

Unique among the nations, America recognized the source of our character as being godly and eternal, not being civic and temporal. And because we have understood that our source is eternal, America has been different. We have no king but Jesus.

—John Ashcroft, in a commencement address at Bob Jones University

The Roman [Catholic] Church is not another Christian denomination. It is a satanic counterfeit, an ecclesiastic tyranny over the souls of men, not to bring them to salvation, but to hold them bound in sin and to hurl them into eternal damnation.

—Bob Jones, Jr., university president, *Faith for the Family* magazine.

Our culture is superior. Our culture is superior because our religion is Christianity and that is the truth that makes men free.

—Pat Buchanan, address to the Christian Coalition.

We should invade their countries, kill their leaders, and convert them to Christianity.

—Ann Coulter, contributing editor to *National Review Online,* responding to the 9/11 attacks

There will never be world peace until God's house
and God's people are given their rightful place
of leadership at the top of the world.

—Pat Robertson

The Bible is the inerrant…word of the living God. It is
absolutely infallible, without error in all matters
pertaining to faith and practice, as well as in
areas such as geography, science, history, etc.

—Jerry Falwell

Those who study jihad will understand why Islam wants to
conquer the whole world. All the countries conquered by
Islam or to be conquered in the future will be marked for
everlasting salvation. For they shall live under [God's law].

**—Ruhollah Khomeini, ayatullah who led
an Islamic revolution in Iran**

I knew my God was bigger than his [God]. I knew
that my God was a real God, and his was an idol.

**—William G. Boykin, U.S. Army Lieutenant General,
in a speech to evangelical Christians describing
his confrontation with a Muslim warlord**

CHRISTIANS AGAINST PLURALISM

Like all idolatries, democratism substitutes a false god for the real, a love of process for a love of country.
—Pat Buchanan, Republican presidential candidate and commentator

The long-term goal of Christians in politics should be to gain exclusive control over the franchise. Those who refuse to submit publicly to the eternal sanctions of God by submitting to His Church's public marks of the covenant—baptism and holy communion—must be denied citizenship, just as they were in ancient Israel.
—Gary North, author of *Political Polytheism: The Myth of Pluralism*

I pledge allegiance to the Christian flag and to the Savior, for whose Kingdom it stands, one Savior, crucified, risen, and coming again, with life and liberty for all who believe.
—Dan Quayle, George H. W. Bush's vice president

The "wall of separation between church and state" is a metaphor based on bad history, a metaphor which has proved useless as a guide to judging. It should be frankly and explicitly abandoned.
—William Rehnquist, chief justice of the U.S. Supreme Court

There is no such thing as separation of church and state in the Constitution. It is a lie of the left and we are not going to take it anymore.
—Pat Robertson

We are approaching a time when Christians, especially, may have to declare the social contract between Enlightenment rationalists and Biblical believers—which formed the basis of the constitution written at our nation's founding—null and void.
—Cal Thomas, conservative columnist

After the Christian majority takes control, pluralism will be seen as immoral and evil and the state will not permit anybody the right to practice evil.
—Gary Potter, president of Catholics for Christian Political Action

CORPORATE AND PERSONAL GREED

The corporation cannot be ethical, its only
responsibility is to make a profit.
—Milton Freidman

The point is that you can't be too greedy.
—Donald Trump, in *Trump: The Art of the Deal*.

ENVIRONMENTAL ABANDONMENT

God says, "Earth is yours. Take it. Rape it. It's yours."
—Ann Coulter

We don't have to protect the environment,
the Second Coming is at hand.
—James Watt, Ronald Reagan's secretary of the interior

GYNEPHOBIA

The real liberators of American women were not the feminist noise-makers, they were the automobile, the supermarket, the shopping center, the dishwasher, the washer-dryer, the freezer.
—Pat Buchanan

God created Adam, lord of all living
creatures, but Eve spoiled it all.
—Martin Luther, the founder of Protestantism

Rail as they will against discrimination, women are simply not endowed by nature with the same measure of single-minded ambition and the will to succeed in the fiercely competitive world of Western capitalism…. The mama bird builds the nest.
—Pat Buchanan

I really believe that the pagans and the abortionists and the feminists and the gays and the lesbians…the ACLU, People for the American Way, all of them who have tried to secularize America, I point the finger in their face and say, "You helped [the September 11 attacks] happen."
—Jerry Falwell

I expect a great reward in heaven.
**—Paul Hill, former minister executed in Florida
for murdering a doctor who performed abortions**

I prefer to call the most obnoxious feminists what they really are:
feminazis…. I often use it to describe women who are obsessed
with perpetuating a modern-day holocaust: abortion.
—Rush Limbaugh

Women's liberation and gay liberation [are] part of the
same thing: a weakening of the moral standards of this nation.
—Nancy Reagan

The feminist agenda is not about equal rights for women. It is
about a socialist, anti-family political movement that encourages
women to leave their husbands, kill their children, practice
witchcraft, destroy capitalism, and become lesbians.
—Pat Robertson

The claim that American women are downtrodden
and unfairly treated is the fraud of the century.
**—Phyllis Schlafly, leader of the Eagle Forum, an organization
originally founded to oppose the Equal Rights Amendment**

Having chicks around is the kind of thing that breaks
up the intense training. It gives you relief, and
then afterward you go back to the serious stuff.
**—Arnold Schwarzenegger, in a magazine
interview on his life as a body-builder**

I think contraception is disgusting—
people using each other for pleasure.
**—Joe Scheidler, director of the
Pro-Life Action League**

HATE & INTOLERANCE

My only regret with Timothy McVeigh is he
did not go to the *New York Times* building.
**—Ann Coulter, on the man who detonated the bomb outside the
Oklahoma City federal office building, killing 168 people**

When I, or people like me, are running the
country, you'd better flee, because we will find
you, we will try you, and we'll execute you.
—Randall Terry, speaking about doctors who perform abortions

[Tolerance is a] kind of watchword of those who reject the concept of right and wrong.... It's a kind of a desensitization to evil of all varieties. Everything has become acceptable to those who are tolerant.

—James Dobson, founder of Focus on Family, the largest international right-wing religious organization in America

I think Mohammed was a terrorist.

—Jerry Falwell

I want you to just let a wave of intolerance wash over you. I want you to let a wave of hatred wash over you. Yes, hate is good.... Our goal is a Christian nation. We have a biblical duty, we are called on by God to conquer this country. We don't want equal time. We don't want pluralism.

—Randall Terry, founder of anti-abortion group Operation Rescue

HOMOPHOBIA

State universities are breeding grounds, quite literally, for sexually transmitted diseases (including HIV), homosexual behavior, unwanted pregnancies, abortions, alcoholism, and drug abuse.

—James Dobson

AIDS is the wrath of a just God against homosexuals.
—Jerry Falwell

[The Tinky Winky Teletubby] is purple—the gay-pride color; and his antenna is shaped like a triangle—the gay-pride symbol.
—Jerry Falwell, raising suspicions about a toy

[T]hese perverted homosexuals ... absolutely hate everything that you and I and most decent, God-fearing citizens stand for…. Make no mistake. These deviants seek no less than total control and influence in society, politics, our schools, and in our exercise of free speech and religious freedom…. If we do not act now, homosexuals will own America!
—Jerry Falwell

We are powerless to act in cases of oral-genital intimacy unless it obstructs interstate commerce.
—J. Edgar Hoover, former FBI director

Those who behave in a homosexual fashion… shall not enter the kingdom of God.
—Pope John Paul II

If the Supreme Court says that you have the right to consensual [gay] sex within your home, then you have the right to bigamy, you have the right to polygamy, you have the right to incest, you have the right to adultery....It all comes from, I would argue, this right to privacy that doesn't exist, in my opinion, in the United States Constitution.

—Rick Santorum, U.S. senator and chairman
of the Republican Senate Caucus

You should only get AIDS and die, you pig!
—Michael Savage, right-wing MSNBC host,
fired after saying this to a gay caller

I think that gay marriage is something that should be between a man and a woman.
—Arnold Schwarzenegger

HYPOCRISY

We will rid the world of the evildoers.
—George W. Bush

The Congress didn't vote themselves a pay raise.... We just simply did not deny ourselves that normal increase in our cost of living that every other worker in America not only expects, but insists upon.
—Dick Armey, House Republican majority leader

I've gambled all my life and it's never been a moral issue with me. I liked church bingo when I was growing up.
—William Bennett, Ronald Reagan's secretary of education and author of *The Book of Virtues*, justifying his multimillion dollar gambling addiction

I'm a uniter, not a divider.
—George W. Bush, made this a central campaign theme in 2000

Too many whites are getting away with drug use....The answer is to go out and find the ones who are getting away with it, convict them, and send them up the river.
—Rush Limbaugh, right-wing radio talk-show host, under investigation for allegedly buying thousands of addictive prescription drugs

INANITY

You're working hard to put food on your families.
—George W. Bush

I've got a record, a record that is conservative
and a record that is compassionated.
—George W. Bush

They misunderestimated me.
—George W. Bush

When the temptation to masturbate is strong, yell "Stop!"
to those thoughts as loudly as you can in your mind.
Then recite a portion of the Bible or sing a hymn.
—Mormon Youth Guide to Self-Control

Guns don't kill people, people do.
**—NRA slogan, obscures the issue of how the
availability of guns facilitates violent crime**

I was recently on a tour of Latin America, and the only
regret I have was that I didn't study Latin harder in
school so I could converse with those people.

—Dan Quayle

Republicans understand the importance
of bondage between a mother and child.

—Dan Quayle

Government is not the solution to our
problems. Government *is* the problem.

**—Ronald Reagan, helping to create the
stereotype of the big-government liberal**

Trees cause more pollution than automobiles do.

—Ronald Reagan

INEPTITUDE

Mathematics are one of the fundamentaries
of educationalizing our youths.

—George W. Bush, in an address to Congress

I think one of the great problems we have in the Republican
Party is that we don't encourage you to be nasty.
—Newt Gingrich, former speaker of the
U.S. House of Representatives

That's not a lie, it's a terminological inexactitude.
—Alexander Haig, Ronald Reagan's secretary of state

Capital punishment is our society's
recognition of the sanctity of human life.
—Orrin Hatch, Republican U.S. senator
explaining his support for the death penalty

I was not lying. I said things that later on seemed to be untrue.
—Richard M. Nixon

I was provided with additional input that was radically different
from the truth. I assisted in furthering that version.
—Oliver North, Reagan administration official in
his Iran-Contra testimony before Congress

I'm not a crook.
**—Richard M. Nixon, defending
himself in the Watergate scandal**

Welcome to President Bush, Mrs. Bush, and my fellow astronauts.
—Dan Quayle, at the twentieth anniversary of the moon landing

What a waste it is to lose one's mind. Or not to have a mind is
being very wasteful. How true that is.
**—Dan Quayle, mangling the slogan from the United Negro
College Fund, "A mind is a terrible thing to waste"**

I believe that people would be alive
today if there were a death penalty.
—Nancy Reagan

My fellow Americans, I am pleased to tell you
I just signed legislation which outlaws Russia
forever. The bombing begins in five minutes.
—Ronald Reagan, said during a radio microphone test

IRAQ WAR

Mission Accomplished

—Banner boasting victory in the war in Iraq was the backdrop to President Bush's speech aboard the USS *Abraham Lincoln*

Intelligence gathered by this and other governments leaves no doubt that the Iraq regime continues to possess and conceal some of the most lethal weapons ever devised.

—George W. Bush

The British government has learned that Saddam Hussein recently sought significant quantities of uranium from Africa [for nuclear weapons].

—George W. Bush included this lie in his 2003 State of the Union address over the objections of the CIA

There are some who feel like that conditions [in Iraq] are such that they can attack us there. My answer is to bring them on.

—George W. Bush, revealing an amazingly cavalier reaction to human lives at risk

We found the weapons of mass destruction.
**—George W. Bush, referring to two tractor-trailers found in
Iraq that had no trace of chemical or biological agents**

From a marketing point of view, you don't
introduce a new product in August.
**—Andrew Card, George W. Bush's chief of staff, explaining
why the Bush administration waited until after Labor Day in
its public relations offensive about the need to invade Iraq**

We will, in fact, be greeted as liberators [in Iraq]…I think it
will go relatively quickly…[in] weeks rather than months.
**—Dick Cheney, vice president and former
head of Halliburton, the recipient of hundreds
of millions of dollars in no-bid contracts in Iraq**

The president of the United States and the secretary of
defense would not assert as plainly and bluntly as they
have that Iraq has weapons of mass destruction if it was
not true, and if they did not have a solid basis for saying it.
**—Ari Fleischer, White House spokesman
for the Bush administration**

We don't do body counts.
—Tommy Franks, U.S. Central Command General, explaining America's attitude toward Iraqi war deaths (by some estimates, 10,000 Iraqi civilians have been killed by U.S. forces)

[The president's] task is not to educate or persuade us. It is to defeat Saddam Hussein. And that will require the president at times to mislead rather than clarify, to deceive rather than to explain.
—William Kristol, editor of *The Weekly Standard* and former chief of staff to Dan Quayle

I think all foreigners should stop interfering in the internal affairs of Iraq.
—Paul Wolfowitz, possibly overlooking the U.S. conquest and occupation of Iraq

I'm not a lawyer. My impression is that what has been charged thus far is abuse, which I believe technically is different from torture.
—Donald Rumsfeld, expressing his view on the rapes, beatings, and sexual humiliation in Iraq's Abu Ghraib prison.

For bureaucratic reasons, we settled on one issue, weapons of mass destruction [to justify the Iraq War], because it was the one reason everyone could agree on.
—Paul Wolfowitz, explaining the Bush administration's rationale for war

This is no different than what happens at the Skull and Bones initiation…I'm talking about people having a good time, these people, you ever heard of emotional release? You [ever] heard of need to blow some steam off?
—Rush Limbaugh's take on the actions of guards who sexually abused and humiliated Iraqi prisoners.

LIBERAL BASHING

Liberals become indignant when you question their patriotism, but simultaneously work overtime to give terrorists a cushion for the next attack and laugh at dumb Americans who love their country and hate the enemy.
—Ann Coulter

The inevitable logic of the liberal position is to be for treason.
—Ann Coulter, from her book all about liberal treachery

We're fighting against humanism, we're fighting against liberalism…we are fighting against all the systems of Satan that are destroying our nation today…our battle is with Satan himself.

—Jerry Falwell, expressing a decidedly unfavorable view of liberal humanism

You are seeing today an all out attempt to marshal the forces of the opposition, using not merely the communists, or their fellow travelers—the deluded liberals, the eggheads, and some of my good friends in both the Democratic and Republican Parties who can become heroes overnight in the eyes of the left-wing press if they will just join with the jackal pack.

—Joseph McCarthy, former Republican U.S. Senator, known for his unsupported accusations of communist infiltration

MEANNESS

The long-term goal [is] the execution of abortionists and parents who hire them. If we argue that abortion is murder, then we must call for the death penalty.

—Gary DeMar, from his book *Ruler of Nations*

If you've seen one city slum you've seen them all.
—Spiro T. Agnew, Richard Nixon's vice president

Please don't kill me.
—George W. Bush, while governor of Texas, mocking a woman's plea for clemency after he decided to put her to death

NEO-FASCISM

[Hitler] was…an individual of great courage, a soldier's soldier in the Great War, a leader steeped in the history of Europe, who possessed oratorical powers that could awe even those who despised him. But Hitler's success was not based on his extraordinary gifts alone. His genius was an intuitive sense of the mushiness, the character flaws, the weakness masquerading as morality that was in the hearts of the statesmen who stood in his path.
—Pat Buchanan

A dictatorship would be a lot easier.
—George W. Bush

We need to execute people like John Walker in order to physically intimidate liberals by making them realize that they could be killed, too. Otherwise they will turn into outright traitors.

—Ann Coulter, referring to the young American who was captured after joining the Taliban

The judges need to be intimidated; they need to uphold the Constitution. If they don't behave, we're going to go after them in a big way.

—Tom DeLay, expressing his attitude toward perceived judicial activism

Democracy used to be a good thing, but now it has gotten into the wrong hands.

—Jesse Helms, former Republican U.S. senator

I want to be invisible. I do guerrilla warfare. I paint my face and travel at night. You don't know it's over until you're in a body bag. You don't know until election night.

—Ralph Reed, former executive director of the Christian Coalition

If Christian people work together, they can succeed during this decade in winning back control of the institutions that have been taken from them over the past seventy years. Expect confrontations that will be not only unpleasant, but at times physically bloody.
—Pat Robertson

I admired Hitler…because he came from being a little man with almost no formal education, up to power. I admire him for being such a good public speaker and for what he did with it.
—Arnold Schwarzenegger

OBTUSENESS

Four-fifths of all our problems would disappear if we would only sit down and keep still.
—Calvin Coolidge, Republican president of
the United States prior to the stock market crash

Grown men should not be having sex with prostitutes unless they are married to them.
—Jerry Falwell

Canada is a left-wing socialist basketcase.
What kind of friends are they?
**—Sean Hannity, co-host of a talk show
on the Fox News Channel**

I want to be sure that he is a ruthless son of a bitch, that he will
do what he is told, that every income tax return I want to see, I
see. That he will go after our enemies and not go after our friends.
Now it's as simple as that. If he isn't, he doesn't get the job.
**—Richard Nixon, on the kind of person he wanted
to head the Internal Revenue Service**

Without censorship, things can get
terribly confused in the public mind.
**—William Westmoreland, U.S. Army
general on the war in Vietnam**

There are known knowns. There are things we know we know.
There are known unknowns; that is to say, we know there are
things we know we don't know. But there are also unknown
unknowns—the ones we don't know we don't know.
—Donald Rumsfeld

Evolution is a bankrupt speculative philosophy, not a scientific fact. Only a spiritually bankrupt society could ever believe it.... Only atheists could accept this satanic theory.
—Jimmy Swaggart

Why should we subsidize intellectual curiosity?
—Ronald Reagan

RACISM

We shall work for the establishment of a separate homeland for African Americans, so each race will be free to pursue its own destiny without racial conflicts or ill will.
—David Duke

[African Americans] are 12 percent of the population. Who the hell cares?
—Rush Limbaugh

Segregation now, segregation tomorrow, and segregation forever!
—George Wallace, inaugural address as governor of Alabama.

Let the unskilled jobs, let the kinds of jobs that take
absolutely no knowledge whatsoever to do—
let stupid and unskilled Mexicans do that work.
—Rush Limbaugh

I want to say this about my state: when Strom Thurmond ran
for president, we voted for him. We're proud of it. And if
the rest of the country had followed our lead, we wouldn't
have had all these problems over all these years, either.
**—Trent Lott, former Republican Senate majority leader,
paying tribute to Thurmond's segregationist candidacy**

I've been to Africa three times. All right? You can't bring
Western reasoning into the culture, the same way
you can't bring it into fundamental Islam.
—Bill O'Reilly

I don't feel we did wrong in taking this great country away from
them. There were great numbers of people who needed new land,
and the Indians were selfishly trying to keep it for themselves.
—John Wayne, movie icon known for playing cowboys

I want to tell you that there's not enough troops in the army to force the Southern people to break down segregation and admit the Negro race into our theaters, into our swimming pools, into our homes and into our churches.
—Strom Thurmond, ran as a third-party candidate for president in 1948 on a segregationist platform

SOCIAL AND ECONOMIC IRRESPONSIBILITY

Reagan proved deficits don't matter.
—Dick Cheney

The idea that a congressman would be tainted by accepting money from private industry or private sources is essentially a socialist argument.
—Newt Gingrich

It is true that if you are poor and can't afford a good lawyer, your odds of going to prison skyrocket. But you know what? Tough!
—Bill O'Reilly

We didn't squander a surplus. We never had it.
—John W. Snow, George W. Bush's treasury secretary

TERRORISM

To those who scare peace-loving people with phantoms of lost liberty, my message is this: your tactics only aid terrorists, for they erode our national unity and diminish our resolve.
—John Ashcroft

FBI Urges Police to Watch for People With Almanacs
—Newspaper headline about an FBI intelligence bulletin inviting police to detain people based on their reading habits

Airports scrupulously apply the same laughably ineffective airport harassment to Suzy Chapstick as to Muslim hijackers. It is preposterous to assume every passenger is a potential crazed homicidal maniac. We know who the homicidal maniacs are.
—Ann Coulter

Even fanatical Muslim terrorists don't hate America like liberals do.
—Ann Coulter

The potential of a weapon of mass destruction and a terrorist, massive, casualty-producing event somewhere in the Western world…[could cause] our population to question our own Constitution and to begin to militarize our country in order to avoid a repeat of another mass casualty-producing event. Which in fact, then begins to unravel the fabric of our Constitution.

—Tommy Franks, the general who led the invasion in Iraq, predicting a doomsday scenario

This crusade, this war on terrorism, is going to take a while. [emphasis added]

—George W. Bush, inviting comparisons to the first Christian crusade on the Muslim world

UNDERMINING PUBLIC EDUCATION

The decline in American pride, patriotism, and piety can be directly attributed to the extensive reading of so-called "science fiction" by our young people.

—Jerry Falwell

We are engaged in a social, political, and cultural war. There's a lot of talk in America about pluralism. But the bottom line is somebody's values will prevail. And the winner gets the right to teach our children what to believe.

—Gary Bauer, former director of the Family Research Council, a fundamentalist Christian advocacy group

The unfortunate truth is that "evolution" has become a controversial buzzword that could prevent some from reading the proposed biology curriculum.

—Kathy Cox, Georgia superintendent of education, explaining why the word "evolution" should be purged from the state curriculum.

As people do better, they start voting like Republicans— unless they have too much education and vote Democratic, which proves there can be too much of a good thing.

—Karl Rove, George W. Bush's chief political handler

The decline in American pride, patriotism, and piety can be directly attributed to the extensive reading of so-called "science fiction" by our young people.

—Jerry Falwell

The public school system is damned. Let me tell you how radical I am. Christian students should be in Christian schools. If you have to sell your car, live in a smaller house, or work a night job, put your child in Christian schools. If you can't afford it, home school.
—Jerry Falwell

Secular schools can never be tolerated because such schools have no religious instruction, and a general moral instruction without a religious foundation is built on air; consequently, all character training and religion must be derived from faith…we need believing people.
—Adolf Hitler

All things equal, I would prefer to have a child in a school that has a strong appreciation for the values of the Christian community, where a child is taught to have a strong faith….That's not the case in a public school where there are so many different kids with different kinds of values.
—Rod Paige, secretary of education, appointed by George W. Bush to advocate for the public schools

I imagine every Christian would agree that we need to remove the humanism from the public schools. There is only one way to accomplish this: to abolish the public schools.
—Robert L. Thoburn, author of *The Children Trap*

UNION DISREGARD

The rights and interests of the laboring man will be protected and cared for not by our labor agitators, but by the Christian men to whom God in his infinite wisdom has given control of property interests of the country.
—George Baer, railroad industrialist

They don't suffer; they can't even speak English.
—George Baer, responding to a reporter's question about impossible living wages and conditions during a coal strike

Labor unions should study and read the Bible instead of asking for more money. When people get right with God, they are better workers.
—Jerry Falwell